CANADA
The Dam!
GRAND COULEE DAM
Spokane
Chelan
Wenatchee
IDAHO
Columbia River
White Bluffs
SNAKE RIVER
Potato Country
Walla Walla
ia River
Arlington, OR
The Dalles, OR
Dee, OR
Parkdale, OR
OREGON

26 SONGS in 30 DAYS

GRAND COULEE HIGHWAY AT EAGLE ROCK - WASH

26 SONGS in 30 DAYS

WOODY GUTHRIE'S
COLUMBIA RIVER SONGS *and the Planned*
Promised Land in the PACIFIC NORTHWEST

GREG VANDY

with **DANIEL PERSON**

SASQUATCH BOOKS
SEATTLE

Printed in China

Published by Sasquatch Books

20 19 18 17 16   9 8 7 6 5 4 3 2 1

Editor: Gary Luke
Production editor: Em Gale
Design: Anna Goldstein
Copyeditor: Elizabeth Johnson
Map on endsheets: Drew Christie

Front cover photographs:
Photo of Woody Guthrie, circa 1939 from the Daily
Worker/Daily World Photo Collection in box 36,
folder 7113; Tamiment Library/Robert F. Wagner
Labor Archives, New York University.
Photo of dam courtesy of the Bureau
of Land Reclamation
Back cover texture: Vadim Georgiev/Shutterstock.com

Library of Congress Cataloging-in-
Publication Data is available.

ISBN: 978-1-57061-970-0

Sasquatch Books
1904 Third Avenue, Suite 710
Seattle, WA 98101
(206) 467-4300
www.sasquatchbooks.com
custserv@sasquatchbooks.com

This book is dedicated to my lovely wife, Jana, for her amazing patience and support of this effort and all my "passion projects" over the years. And to my brother Mark, who was my first inspiration on the path of music discovery and the experience of being a fan, always and forever.

CONTENTS

Preface xi

CHAPTER 1: Biggest Thing That Man Has Ever Done 1

CHAPTER 2: Hard Travelin' 15

CHAPTER 3: Ballad of the Great Grand Coulee 33

CHAPTER 4: Ramblin' Blues (New York Town) 47

CHAPTER 5: Pastures of Plenty 63

CHAPTER 6: Ramblin' Blues (Portland Town) 91

CHAPTER 7: Roll, Columbia, Roll 115

CHAPTER 8: Oregon Trail 131

CHAPTER 9: Talkin' Columbia 147

Acknowledgments 155
Discography 159
Bibliography 173
Photo Credits 181
Index 185

WOODY GUTHRIE'S COLUMBIA RIVER SONGS

Ballad of Jackhammer John

Biggest Thing That Man Has Ever Done

Columbia Waters

Eleckatricity and All

End of My Line

Grand Coulee Dam

Grand Coulee Powder Monkey

Guys on the Grand Coulee Dam

Hard Travelin'

It Takes a Married Man to Sing a Worried Song

Jackhammer Blues

Lumber Is King

New Found Land

Oregon Trail

Out Past the End of the Line

Pastures of Plenty

Portland Town to Klamath Falls

Ramblin' Blues

Rumblin' Round

Roll On, Columbia

Roll, Columbia, Roll

Talkin' Blues

Columbia Talkin' Blues

Song of the Grand Coulee Dam

Washington Talkin' Blues

White Ghost Train

ROLL ON COLUMBIA, ROLL ON
Comp. —(By Woody Guthrie)

Green Douglas Fir where the waters cut through,
Down her wild mountains and canyons she flew,
Canadian Northwest to the Ocean so blue,
It's roll on Columbia, Roll on!

    Roll On, Columbia, roll on!
    Roll On, Columbia, roll on!
    Your Power is turning our Darkness to Dawn;
    Roll on, Columbia, Roll on!
Other great rivers add power to you,
Yakima, Snake, and the Klickitat, too,
Willamette, Sandy, and Hood River, too;
Roll on Columbia, roll on! (Chorus if desired)

It's there on your banks that we fought many a fight,
Sheridan's boys in the block house that night,
They saw us in death, but never in flight;
Roll on, Columbia, roll on! (Chorus if desired)

Our loved ones we lost there at Coe's little store,
By fireball and rifle, a dozen or more,
We won by the Mary and soldiers she bore;
Roll on, Columbia, roll on! (Chorus if desired)

Remember the trial when the battle was won,
The wild Indian warriors to the tall timber run,
We hung every Indian with smoke in his gun;
Roll on, Columbia, roll on! (Chorus if desired)

Year after year we had tedious trials,
Fighting the rapids at Cascades and Dalles,
The Injuns rest peaceful on Memaloose Isle;
Roll on, Columbia, roll on! (Chorus if desired)

At Bonneville now there are ships in the locks,
The waters have risen and cleared all the rocks,
Ship loads of plenty will steam past the docks,
So roll on, Columbia, roll on! (Chorus if desired).

And on up the river at Grand Coulee dam,
The mightiest thing ever built by a man,
To run the great factories for old Uncle Sam;
It's roll on, Columbia, roll on!

    (Notice: The chorus of this song can be sung after every
    verse, or after every two or three verses, as you like.
    This song was wrote up by an Oakie passing through your
    country, and I'm pretty certain that everybody just
    first a coming into this country has got some such similar
    song in his or her head, but times is such that they just
    dont sing it out loud, so you might not hear it.
    Woody Guthrie, outskirts of Portland, Oregon, 5-12-1941.)

PREFACE

The story of Woody Guthrie and the Columbia River is now in its fourth generation. In its first iteration—directly after Guthrie visited the Northwest and wrote his songs—it seemed a story hardly worth telling. Guthrie wasn't well-known, and the film that his songs were supposed to be used for ended up being postponed on account of World War II.

The second generation of the story came of age in the early 1960s, when several of Guthrie's Columbia River ballads entered mainstream culture via the folk-music revival sweeping the nation. The fact that folkies across the country were singing about the Grand Coulee Dam in songs like "Pastures of Plenty" spurred an Associated Press writer in Portland named Gordon Macnab to do some digging at the headquarters of the Bonneville Power Administration, resulting in a national wire story relating that Guthrie had been hired by the agency to write ballads about the river for a film it was making. But the story of Woody and the BPA soon fell back into obscurity.

The third generation came about in the 1980s, when an audiovisual specialist for the BPA named Bill Murlin happened upon the documentary the agency eventually made using Guthrie's songs. A folksinger himself, Murlin was surprised to see in the credits that the public information office he was employed by had once had the preeminent folksinger of the twentieth century on the payroll.

Over the next decade, Murlin completed invaluable research that significantly augmented what we now know about Guthrie's time in our region. Murlin conducted extensive interviews with people who worked with Woody at the BPA—the most important being his boss, Stephen Kahn, and Elmer Buehler, who drove the folksinger up and down the Columbia River. Murlin also completed the previously neglected task of tracking down the recordings Guthrie had made in the BPA's basement-closet studio. That effort uncovered several never-before-heard recordings, including one of him singing his most famous Columbia River ballad, "Roll On, Columbia." Until Murlin's discovery, it was assumed that there was no recording of Guthrie singing that song. It isn't a stretch to suggest that had Murlin not discovered it, the single copy that existed in 1985 would have been lost to history.

Today, all of the people who knew Woody Guthrie's Columbia River story firsthand have passed away. Greg was fortunate to interview Elmer Buehler in 2008, for a radio special on Seattle's KEXP, but we have had to partially rely on interviews conducted by others, including Bill Murlin and documentary filmmakers Michael Madjic and Michael O'Rourke. For us and our editor, this raised the obvious questions: What did we have to add? Why tell the story yet another time?

Two answers emerged. First, while extensive research into Guthrie's time in the Northwest had been conducted, we found that all the books about the singer to date offer scant treatment of the material. Guthrie lived a full life, and we don't fault his biographers for not dwelling on his monthlong sojourn in our region. Rather, we are indebted to them for their excellent scholarship, especially Ed Cray and Joe Klein. However, as Guthrie himself put it, "When a song or a ballad mentions the name of a river, a town, a spot, a fight, or the sound of somebody's name that you know and are familiar with, there is a sort of quiet kind of pride come up through your blood." As writers who sang "Roll On, Columbia" in grade school and have bundled up to watch the laser light show at the Grand Coulee Dam, we feel that quiet pride every time we hear Guthrie sing "In the misty crystal glitter of the wild and windward spray," and we wanted to share it.

More importantly, seventy-five years after Woody Guthrie was hired by the BPA, the impulse behind his Columbia River ballads is deeply misunderstood, if understood at all. Today, the engineering of the Columbia Basin that was just beginning during Guthrie's trip to the region is considered a mixed blessing at best. The decimation of the once-bountiful salmon runs and the disposition of Native American culture and land rightly cast a pall over the dams. While it's wise to occasionally reassess the value of any human endeavor, hindsight can also distort history, and this seems to be the case with Guthrie's legacy in the Northwest.

When he was employed by the BPA, he was less than a year removed from his stint writing for a Communist Party newspaper. And according to Elmer Buehler, he colorfully shunned an invitation from the chamber of commerce in Spokane, stating that he'd never support such an organization.

Yet today, Guthrie's songs are apt to be celebrated by pro-dam business interests and dismissed by environmentalists as propaganda for an ecological disaster. Best-selling author David James Duncan, in his 2002 book of essays, *My Story as Told by Water*, writes that Guthrie was "dutifully whipping off a few industrial river ditties . . . never once suspecting the rash of Manifest Destinarian bronzes and Tourist Brainwashing kiosks that would one day immortalize his sweet face and no-brainer lyrics."

The record needs correcting. Guthrie wasn't a pro-business hack; he didn't set out to write "industrial river ditties," and his lyrics are certainly not "no-brainers." This book doesn't seek to either defend or condemn the Columbia River projects. But it does attempt to prove beyond a doubt to twenty-first-century readers that Woody Guthrie's enthusiasm for the Grand Coulee and Bonneville Dams was genuine and, indeed, inspiring.

Like the Columbia itself, this story starts in many streams: the fight for public power in Washington and Oregon; the plight of farmers in the drought-stricken Dust Bowl; a crazy scheme to irrigate the Washington desert; and the sudden rise of World War II industries in

Seattle and Portland. Where they all converge is a collection of twenty-six songs written in thirty days that attest to the worth and aspirations of the American workingman. Put in their proper context, songs like "Pasture of Plenty" and "Grand Coulee Dam" cease to be merely catchy folk tunes. Instead, they present a powerful thesis: that the American worker, given the opportunity, has the power to turn deserts into orchards, and rivers into a force strong enough to defeat Nazi Germany. They are a deeply patriotic salvo from a man whose patriotism would wrongly be questioned. They are a refutation to anyone who suggests that the government doesn't have any business helping the common man. The songs are also an optimistic answer to the despairing questions that arose from the Dust Bowl. In fact, what we have come to realize is that Woody Guthrie's Columbia River songs are a direct answer to his Dust Bowl ballads.

We feel deeply that this is a story worth telling again because Woody's message is one worth hearing again.

—GREG VANDY AND DANIEL PERSON, SEATTLE, 2016

The Biggest Thing That Man Ever Done

I'm just a Lonesome Traveler, the great Historical Bum,
I'm highly educated and from History I have come;
I built the Rock of Ages, 'twas in the year of One,
And that was about the biggest thing that Man had ever done.

I worked in the Garden of Eden, 'twas in the year of Two,
Join'd the Apple Pickers Union, I always paid my due;
I'm the man that signed the contract to raise the rising Sun,
And that was about the biggest thing that Man had ever done.

I was straw boss on the Pyramids, the Tower of Babel, too,
I opened up the ocean, let the Migrant Children through;
I fought a million battles and I never lost a one,
Well, that was about the biggest thing that Man had ever done.

I beat the daring Roman, I beat the daring Turk,
I defeated Nero's army with thirty minutes work;
I stopped the mighty Kaiser, and stopped the mighty Hun;
And That was about the biggest thing that Man had ever done.

I was in the Revolution when we set the country free,
Me and a couple of Indians that dumped the Boston Tea;
We won the battle at Valley Forge, and battle of Bull Run,
And that was about the biggest thing that Man had ever done.

Next we won the Slavery War, some other folks and me,
And every Slave in Dixie was freed by Robert Lee,
The Slavery Men had lost the War, the Freedom Men had won;
And that was about the biggest thing that Man had ever done.

And then I took to farming on the great midwestern plain,
The dust it blowed a hundred years, but never come a rain;
Well, me and a million other folks we left there on the run,
And that was about the biggest thing that Man had ever done.

I clumb the rocky canyon where the Columbia River rolls,
Seen the salmon leaping the rapids and the falls;
The big Grand Coulee Dam in the State of Washington
Is just about the biggest thing that Man has ever done.

There's a building in New York that you call the Empire State,
I rode the rods to Frisco to walk the Golden Gate,
I've seen every foot of film that Hollywood has run,
But Coulee is the biggest thing that Man has ever done.

Three times the size of Boulder, or the highest Pyramid,
It makes the Tower of Babel a plaything for a kid,
From the rising of the River to the setting of the Sun,
The Coulee is the biggest thing that Man has ever done.

I better quit my talking 'cause I told you all I know,
But please remember, pardner, wherever you may go,
I been from here to yonder, I been from Sun to Sun,
But Coulee Dam's th' biggest thing that Man has ever done.

Woody Guthrie

"Biggest Thing That Man Has Ever Done" Words and Music by Woody Guthrie. WGP/TRO-Ludlow Music Inc. © Copyright 1961, 1963, 1976 (copyrights renewed). Woody Guthrie Publications, Inc. & Ludlow Music, Inc., New York, NY (administered by Ludlow Music, Inc.)

CHAPTER 1

BIGGEST THING THAT MAN HAS EVER DONE

I n the spring of 1941, more than a decade into the Great Depression and less than a year before the attack on Pearl Harbor, America was a nation in transition.

A huge ramp-up of war production across the United States had already changed the very character of the country as it sent warships and bombers across the Atlantic to help the Allies fight Adolf Hitler. At the same time, the dispossessed masses of the economic collapse of the 1930s remained a reality in urban centers and drought-stricken farms alike. For this brief moment, Rosie the Riveter and Tom Joad stood side by side in American consciousness.

Portland, Oregon, exhibited this duality perfectly. Sitting at the confluence of the Columbia and Willamette Rivers, Portland had long been a substantial port city. However, it was chiefly an agricultural port for most of its history, the shipping point for the huge amounts of timber harvested from the thick Pacific Crest forests around it.

That fact changed dramatically in 1940, when the city was chosen as the site of two major shipyards to produce steel "Liberty ships" for Allied forces in Europe. The shipyards sat on either side of the Columbia, just west of where Interstate 5 now crosses the mighty river.

More than a hundred thousand people moved to Portland during the war years. The first ship to roll off the Oregon Shipbuilding Corporation's docks was the *Star of Oregon*, in the fall of 1941, with 454 more to follow in the next four years.

Building of a Liberty ship at a Portland shipyard, 1942

And yet the Depression was still very much alive in Portland. Three miles away from the shipyards sat Sullivan's Gulch, at that time a sprawling Hooverville filled with families left out of work by the economic downturn, which had proven devastating to the timber industry. Houses were made of cardboard, and heat was provided by small fires—"the Depression at its worse," one observer said.

Sitting between these two worlds, both literally and figuratively, was the Bonneville Power Administration. In the literal sense, the BPA was a new agency headquartered in a single-story concrete building at 811 NE Oregon Street in Portland, just five blocks from Sullivan's Gulch and not much farther from the shipyards. In a figurative sense, the BPA was an agency born out of the Great Depression, which proved instrumental during the war.

Created in 1937, the BPA was a novel, perhaps even radical, concept: a federal agency that would sell the power created by federal dams at Grand Coulee and Bonneville in order to drive down the price of electricity. As stated by President Franklin D. Roosevelt and others, its purpose was to weaken private businesses that sold electricity for profit—one of many bold attempts by the Roosevelt administration to fundamentally reshape America's economy.

Predictably, the agency made plenty of well-heeled enemies. The idea of the government controlling the supply of anything, even something like electricity, struck many as socialism. If the government socialized power, what else might go?

"The next thing they'll do is socialize the grocery store, and then they'll socialize your wife, and it's going to be the Russian system coming over and taking over" was a common sentiment the BPA's public information officer Stephen Kahn recalled hearing at town hall meetings when the government tried to sell the idea of a federal power administration in the Pacific Northwest.

BPA promotional poster, circa 1940

That sort of sentiment was frustrating to Kahn. As he saw it, the BPA was part of a massive effort to change the region for the better. Not only were the federal dams and the BPA driving down the cost of electricity—rates dropped by half in some cases—but they were also putting thousands of men to work and providing electricity to factories like the Kaiser shipyards, which employed thousands more. He foresaw irrigation coming off the Grand Coulee Dam and turning vast tracts of the Columbia Basin desert into arable land. He foresaw farmers who'd lost their land in the Depression working that land.

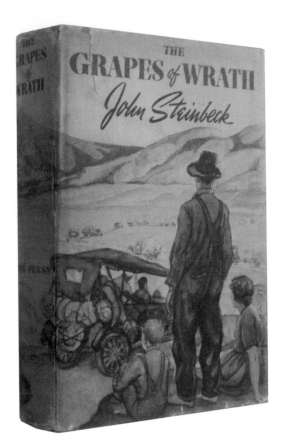

First-edition cover, 1939

As the head of public information for the BPA, Kahn was largely responsible for making people appreciate these benefits, but in 1941, he wasn't sure the message was getting through. The agency had released charts and figures that explained how a publicly controlled power system worked in consumers' favor. However, Kahn decided that in order for people to really get behind it, they shouldn't simply understand the benefits; they should connect with them on an emotional level. What the BPA needed, he decided, was a feature-length film. It would be shown in cinemas across the country in order to do what the recent film adaptation of John Steinbeck's 1939 novel *The Grapes of Wrath* had done: "capture the hearts of people." It wouldn't simply discuss the agency's mission of selling cheap power, but it would show the high stakes and drama of giving citizens control over their own electricity.

In many ways, 1941 was an auspicious time for the government to make such a movie. The New Deal had prompted an unprecedented amount of government-funded artwork through the 1930s. Departing from the urbane tastes of the 1920s, artists sought to tell the story of the common man. In literature, film, and music, the working class was the hero of a newly imagined America. Radio programs featured folksingers, and Hollywood movies had everyday joes like Jimmy Stewart's Mr. Smith facing down corruption in the highest echelons of American power. The 1941 Academy Award for best director went to John Ford for *The Grapes of Wrath*. A popular sentiment of the moment was that we the people, as John Steinbeck had put it in the novel, may in fact be sharing "one big soul."

It was natural, then, that when deciding how to sell the public on the BPA, Kahn started thinking about using a folksinger—someone who would bring the common touch, someone who would turn citizens into true believers in the Columbia River projects. In other words, Kahn needed someone to spread propaganda.

But who?

With that question in mind, Kahn called the preeminent expert on folk music in the United States: twenty-six-year-old Alan Lomax, the assistant in charge at the Archive of American Folk Song at the Library of Congress. Lomax had met folk artists from across the country and recorded everyone from Jelly Roll Morton to Aunt Molly Jackson to Huddie Ledbetter (a.k.a. Lead Belly).

When asked if he knew anyone who might be able to sing for and narrate a film about the Columbia River, Lomax nearly jumped through the line. "I got your man for ya!"

———

In early 1941, that man was broke, busted, and disgusted.

Woody Guthrie was twenty-eight years old, married with three children, and living hand to mouth in Los Angeles. He had one record to his name, which wasn't selling, and had just quit a lucrative gig at CBS in New York. He'd already written most of the lyrics to the song that would define him to generations of Americans—"From the red wood forest to the Gulf Stream waters . . ."—but he hadn't yet put "This Land Is Your Land" onto a record. His marriage was falling apart, he was drinking heavily, and he was seriously behind on his car payments and rent.

The house he and his young family rented on Preston Avenue in Los Angeles's Echo Park neighborhood was dreary and leaky. In a letter to his friend and booster Lomax, Guthrie called it "rambling, rotten, rundown,

Alan Lomax,
circa 1940

rusty . . . Hard to get into. Hard to pay rent on. Hard to get out of." But, he added, "3 kids has got to live in a house." The house belonged to an anarchist poet who'd left it abandoned when she moved to Pasadena, and Woody had worked out a deal that let them stay there free for two months if he painted it. When that time was up, he quickly fell behind on his ten-dollar-per-month rent.

When the Guthries moved in, they couldn't afford furniture, forcing Woody's wife, Mary, to cull what she could from other families' cast-offs. They had trouble putting food on the table, and relied on the charity of neighbors to feed the kids at times.

For Woody's part, he was working itinerantly at best. The only place he seemed to be able to make anything singing was on Skid Row, where he sang for nickels and beer, and that certainly didn't help matters. Friends recalled Guthrie drinking himself into depressive fits in those early months of 1941. Neighbors heard bitter arguments between Woody and Mary. At one point, they said, the family fled as Guthrie hurled empty beer bottles through the windows of their dilapidated house.

He was "in the worst mood I had ever seen him in," friend and neighbor Ed Robbin told Guthrie biographer Ed Cray. "He was very depressed, unhappy, angry and drinking."

At the urging of Lomax, he was plucking away at his autobiography, *Bound for Glory*, an effort that did nothing to help fill the kitchen pantry.

KFVD, the radio station that had first hired Woody years before, put him back on the air, but without pay, and without sponsors to underwrite the show.

Given his destitute situation, it was hard to believe that the last six months of the previous year had proven to be the most lucrative of his career.

In early 1940, Guthrie had moved to New York, where he quickly became a minisensation as a radio personality. After his first appearance on national radio, he was a regular on national and local stations. He performed on the pilot of a radio show Alan Lomax was creating for CBS. And he scored his first hit, thanks to an appearance on WNYC's *Adventures in Music*. It was on that show that he performed his *Grapes of Wrath* ballad, "Tom Joad"—a song that captures the entire saga of John Steinbeck's masterpiece in a few stanzas.

In September of 1940, the Model Tobacco Company invited Guthrie to become the host of a radio program called *Pipe Smoking Time*. It was a typical variety show of the era—conservative, simple, and designed to sell the sponsor's product. The producers wanted Woody to give folksy pitches of tobacco. They even created a theme song based on Woody's signature song, "So Long, It's Been Good to Know Yuh," essentially changing it into a jingle:

> *Howdy, friend. Well, it's sure good to know you.*
> *Load up your pipe and take your life easy.*
> *With Model Tobacco to light up your way,*
> *We'll be glad to be with you today.*

The money was like nothing Woody had ever experienced—his salary was more than $350 a week, which translates to nearly $5,000 in 2016 dollars.

Biggest Thing That Man Has Ever Done

"These folks are paying me so much I have to back a truck up to the pay window to get my money," he shared in a letter—surely to instill confidence in his career choice.

However, for the first time in his life, Guthrie was stifled, forced to limit his creativity. He struggled with the overt commerciality of the show and rules about what he could and couldn't do. Mostly, he just wanted to sing his own songs. But Model wanted him to sing hillbilly songs, he complained to Lomax, songs that made fun of poor folks rather than celebrate them. And everything was scripted. The show had no room for Woody's ad libs, jokes, and topical commentary—lest it strike the listeners at home as something that hinted at Guthrie's far-left political leanings. He grew tired of the shilling and the shallow, demeaning portrayal of his country folk on the airwaves. It was not the place for him. So Woody Guthrie walked away.

He left New York two days after New Year's Day 1941. *Pipe Smoking Time* had been on the air for little more than a month when Guthrie instructed Mary to pack up the kids. He was done with New York and ready to get back to Los Angeles. Loading his family into his new blue Pontiac, one of the only luxuries he would ever buy (on credit), Woody drove to Washington, DC, then down through the southern states to El Paso to visit family, and then out to California. Giving up reasonable stability and a healthy income, they were on the move again. They were always on the move.

As she left the apartment in New York, Mary couldn't have known exactly what awaited her. Still, she must have feared the worst: less work, more poverty, a leaky house they couldn't pay rent on.

Then, out of nowhere, opportunity stopped by the Guthrie household.

It was April, and a man that Woody referred to as "some feller from the Dept. of Interior" came by to chat with him about a film being shot along the Columbia River in Oregon and Washington State. That "feller"

Woody Guthrie performing on the radio program Back Where I Come From *on WABC-CBS Radio, NYC, 1940*

was Gunther von Fritsch, a Hollywood producer who had signed on with Kahn to make the documentary for the BPA. Von Fritsch told Guthrie they were interested in hiring him for a year to act and narrate in the film, as well as write some songs about the river and its federal projects.

The prospect must have been highly exciting to the unemployed Guthrie. But in a letter, he was understated.

"Hope they give me a job," Woody wrote a friend about the episode.

However, a follow-up letter from von Fritsch tempered those hopes, saying that funding for the film was still up in the air and telling him to hang tight.

But Guthrie couldn't hang tight.

The house they were renting turned out to have bad plumbing, and Guthrie seemed intent on making it worse.

As it happened, Mary's brother Fred Jennings and his wife were visiting the Guthries when the "sewer went bad," as Jennings later put it to Ed Cray. In lieu of hiring help with money he didn't have, Guthrie went to get a pickax to see what he could do himself about the backup, Jennings recalled.

"The thing to do is just to dig it up and knock a hole in it with a pick," Guthrie reasoned aloud to his brother-in-law.

Borrowing the tool from a neighbor, he began digging up the crab-grass yard in search of the malfunctioning pipe. If Mary was watching and had any understanding of plumbing, then she surely recognized that with every heave of the pick, any chance of them remaining in their Preston Avenue house grew dimmer.

Pick, pick, pick. Woody hit pay dirt. As could have been predicted, once the pipe was severed, sewage began spilling into the yard. He and his brother-in-law tried to stanch the flow of feces with the grass they'd just dug up, but there was no stopping it.

"Turds were just floating out of it," Jennings recalled.

Seeing they now had a bigger problem on their hands than just a clogged pipe, the Guthries and Jenningses did what they felt was the

practical thing: they abandoned the house. They strapped a mattress on the car, stuffed everyone in, and headed north—homeless again, and no richer than when the day started.

This was the boom-and-bust lifestyle of Woody Guthrie in April 1941. He was the provider for three children and couldn't provide. He was a singer of folk songs who couldn't find his folks anymore. He was a poet deeply connected to the land he stood on who couldn't find any land of his own.

It was because of the broken pipe and the abandoned house that a May 1 follow-up letter airmailed to Guthrie from Portland, addressed to the Preston Avenue house, didn't immediately find him.

The certified letter stated in formal language that Guthrie was being considered for a yearlong position with the Bonneville Power

Woody Guthrie with Maxine "Lefty Lou" Crissman, Mary Guthrie (foreground), and the Jennings family at Preston House, 1941

Administration, and asked that he fill out a series of paperwork to be further considered for the job.

Goings had become even tougher for the Guthrie family. After decamping LA, they'd relocated to an old California gold-mining town named, oddly enough, Columbia. The room that Woody moved his young family into had no power, and he was scraping together money by cutting firewood in the mountains and hauling it into town in his Pontiac—a car less than a year old that was in serious threat of being repossessed. It must have been a sight: Guthrie—all of five foot eight, scrawny as a scarecrow, and having spent his life ducking manual labor—playing lumberjack in the mountains with a new sedan. Although Woody tried as always to put a positive spin on his life in the

Sierra Nevadas—"I'd ruther raise my kids like a herd of young antelope out here in the fresh air" than in the low-rent district of New York City, he told a friend—lumberjacking from his Pontiac wasn't going to cut it for long.

When the BPA letter finally reached the family in Columbia, it probably should have struck Woody Guthrie as, at best, hopeful—a step toward a job sometime down the line. After all, what he needed was work right then.

But Woody Guthrie never saw things the way other people did.

With mere confirmation that there still was a movie in the works along the Columbia River, the family was loaded into the car again—this time headed for Portland. And why not? Woody Guthrie didn't have much else to lose.

HARD TRAVELIN'

By Woody Guthrie

I been a havin' some hard travelin'
I thought you knowed,
I been a havin' some hard travelin'
Way down **th'** road,
    I been a havin' some hard travelin'
    Hard ramblin', hard gamblin',
    I been a havin' some hard travelin', Lord.

I been a hittin' some hard rock minin'
I thought you knowed,
I been a leanin' on a pressure drill
Way down th' road,
    Hammer flyin', air hose a suckin'
    Six foot of mud an' I shore been a muckin'
    I been a havin' some hard travelin', Lord.

I been a hittin' your Pittsburgh steel
I thought you knowed,
I been a pourin' red hot slag
Way down th' road,
    I been a blastin', I been a firin'
    I been a pourin' red hot iron
    I been a havin' some hard travelin', Lord.

I been a hittin' some hard harvestin'
I thought you knowed,
North Dakota to th' Rio Grande
Way down th' road,
    Orchard, field, an' stackin' that hay
    Tryin' give my woman a dollar a day
    I been a havin' some hard travelin', Lord.

I been a hittin' that #1 Highway
I thought you knowed,
I been a poundin' that 66
Way down th' road,
    Workin' on th' farm, workin' in town
    My hands is blistered from my elbows down
    I been a havin' some hard travelin', Lord.

# # #

CHAPTER 2

HARD TRAVELIN'

When you think of the classic folk musician with guitar and harmonica rack, hat, work clothes, and a point of view, you're imagining Woody Guthrie. The man who told you something you already knew. An iconic American figure who became a legend by singing songs simply.

Guthrie will always be a symbol of hard times and Depression-era politics, forever representing the twentieth-century folk identity. His genius was to simplify. He tackled the big subjects with an aw-shucks sensibility that proved to be a gift. He wrote, sang, talked, laughed, and borrowed using an American vernacular that expressed the voice of the people—a theme from which he never wavered. Woody's message was wrapped up in a unique set of beliefs and politics that merged his religious background with a new brand of Americanism layered in modern socialism, with determination to help the poor and the down-and-out.

And yet he was flawed man, with a lifestyle and pattern of bewildering decisions that can be described as selfish and irresponsible, bordering on self-destructive. Some said he had more interest in people in the abstract than the people in his own life. His ramblin' was renowned, and his commitment to the road would ultimately verify his authenticity as someone who knew the land and its people.

He summed up his ethos as an artist simply: "All you can write is what you see."

Naturally, his ramblin' frustrated people close to him, made him a completely unfit father at times, and created a strain on his marriage.

"He could not care less where he spent the night or where he was going the next day," Mary recalled of her folksinger husband decades later. "He was for the downtrodden, but as far as something for himself or his family, it didn't make that much difference."

But Woody would always ramble—in with the dust and out with the wind.

Whatever the cause of his deep restlessness, Woody Guthrie knew homelessness as a young man.

Woodrow Wilson Guthrie was born July 14, 1912, just twelve days after his namesake won the Democratic nomination for president. Woody, as he was quickly nicknamed, was the third child of Charley and Nora Guthrie, and at birth seemed destined to enjoy a comfortable middle-class upbringing. Guthrie's hometown of Okemah, Oklahoma, was a small town on a rocky hill that never quite lived up to its boosters' aspirations—"The town didn't amount to much except on a Saturday, when the farm people would come in there to have a trade day," Woody Guthrie later said. Still, the town was the county seat of Okfuskee County, making it the area's center of commerce and politics, two topics of great interest to Woody's father.

As his son's name suggested, Charley Guthrie was a staunch Democrat. Charley read law as a young man and, with the help of party machine politics, was elected district court clerk for Okfuskee County in 1908, just a year after Oklahoma became a state.

Like the rest of Oklahoma, the county had seen a rush of land settlement after the government opened it up to homesteading in 1889, having previously been reserved for Native American tribes. The famous Oklahoma "Sooners" planted wheat, corn, and—around Woody's hometown

Woody Guthrie illustration for Bound for Glory
depicting Okemah, Oklahoma, 1942

of Okemah—cotton in the parched grassland, trying to make a go of crops in what was, at best, marginal farmland. In the decades after the Sooners arrived, difficult farming conditions led many families into a vicious cycle of debt that caused them to lose their farms and become simple tenants on the land they once owned. Those who had never had land to begin with were faced with low wages that offered little prospect of upward mobility.

These economic factors—all present a generation before the Dust Bowl and the Great Depression—fostered a healthy strain of socialism among Oklahoma's residents. Drawing off meek-shall-inherit-the-earth Bible scripture and antipathy toward banks and railroads, the Socialist Party was able to pull 15 percent of the presidential vote in Okfuskee County in 1912.

However, no such left-leaning ideas entered the Guthrie home at the time. As the Socialists gained popularity around him, Charley in 1912 published columns in the local newspaper mocking their positions, at times engaging in blatantly racist appeals to the white citizens of Okemah. "Socialism Urges Negro Equality" read one of his headlines, aimed at alarming anyone who considered voting Socialist.

Indeed, Charley Guthrie and his young family seemed entirely removed from the plights of the poor farmers in the area—both economically and physically. Even before running for office, Charley became involved in real estate, and he earned enough money from his dealings to buy the first car in Okemah in 1909. And the Guthries were city folk: Charley ran his business out of an office above a bank downtown, and his growing family lived in town.

"We wasn't in that class that John Steinbeck called the Okies," Woody Guthrie later said.

"Papa went to town and made real estate deals with other people, and he brought their money home. Mama could sign a check for any amount, buy every little thing that her eyes like the looks of. [My brother and sister] Roy and Clara could stop off in any store in Okemah and buy new clothes to fit the weather, new things to eat to make you healthy, and Papa was proud because we could all have anything we saw."

Music was a staple in the Guthrie household: Charley liked square-dancing calls and black labor songs; Nora preferred parlor songs like "Gypsy Davy." Like many rural adults, the old-timers of the extended Guthrie family had played music as a hobby and as a way to entertain themselves in the days before radio and records, and they still played for each other in their parlors and on their porches. Woody was born into such an environment. He enjoyed his father's playing and his mother's singing, and learned the old songs in such a way.

The Guthrie family's fortune was further improved by World War I, which proved to be a huge boon to Oklahoma. In an effort to boost wheat production, the US government subsidized the price to keep it selling at two dollars a bushel. This led to a new land rush, as war speculators poured into the area, busting up fragile, dusty soil in search of any land that could support the lucrative crop. For Charley Guthrie's extensive real estate holdings, it meant even better times—and even more impetus to buy Oklahoma farmland on speculation. At the beginning of the 1920s, Charley Guthrie stood as a wealthy man.

It seems impossible to imagine that Woodrow Wilson Guthrie would have become a champion of the workingman had his life continued the way it started for his first eight years. But with the new decade came drastic and devastating changes for the Guthrie family.

With every boom comes a bust, and in the early 1920s the Guthrie family was not immune. When the high wheat prices prompted by the war returned to peacetime prices, tenant farmers working Charley Guthrie's land began defaulting. This left Charley overextended with the banks and forced him to sell off his holdings at fire-sale prices.

Woody Guthrie later said his father lost $50,000 over the course of 1921 and 1922, and pronounced dramatically: "I'm the only man in this world that's lost a farm a day in thirty days."

Meanwhile, the behavior of his mother, which had long been odd and erratic, became something altogether frightening. From early on in Woody's childhood, Nora had wavered between aloofness and violent outbursts. In 1919, she and Woody's older sister, Clara, got into a terrible argument, during which Clara accidentally set herself on fire and ultimately died. It devastated the Guthrie family and would be something that Woody never forgot. In the eyes of her neighbors, the incident cast a pall over Nora, but by the mid-1920s it was clear to Woody that his mother was suffering from severe mental illness. At one point, she left her three-year-old daughter, Mary Jo, to wander the streets downtown while she watched a movie, and she was prone to spastic arm movements that haunted young Woody. Then, on June 25, 1927, when Woody was fourteen, his father was severely burned in a fire. Even Charley never got the story straight as to what happened to him, but it was widely believed that Nora had set him alight in a fit of rage. Two days later she was committed to an insane asylum. Woody visited her there once before she died and was buried in an unmarked grave in 1929.

With his father broken financially and his mother mentally, Guthrie was left to find his own way starting at a young age. For a time he took odd jobs and slept where he could as he traveled in the summers to different parts of Oklahoma and Texas, hitchhiking with his harmonica and singing for nickels and dimes.

He said he learned how to play the "French harp"—or harmonica—when he was fifteen or sixteen years old after hearing a black shoeshiner play a blues song on the instrument.

"I was passing a barbershop one day . . . and there was a big barefooted boy who had his feet turned up toward me, and he was playing the 'Railroad Blues,'" Woody said, telling Alan Lomax about the man who taught him his first harmonica song—following the racist custom of referring to an adult black man as "boy." "It was on a warm summer day, and he was laying there . . . and I says, 'Boy, that's undoubtedly the lonesomest piece of music I've ever run onto in my life. Where in the world did you learn it?' And he say, 'I just lay here listening to the railroad whistle, and whatever it say, I say too.'"

After that first meeting, Guthrie said, he'd stop by every day and ask the man to play the song, which he never played the same way twice—a folk-music tradition that Guthrie fully employed once he learned to play.

In 1929, Woody moved from Okemah to Pampa, a small town in the panhandle of Texas, where his father had moved following the latest boom. This time it was oil. He took a job as a soda jerk at Shorty Harris's drugstore and helped his scarred father run a flophouse. It was Prohibition, and Woody capitalized by serving "jake," pot liquor, and "canned heat" at the purported drugstore, helping the boomtown rats with what ailed them.

But Pampa wouldn't provide any real stability. When the stock market crashed in October 1929, oil briefly sustained the town. Soon enough, though, economic malaise hit, and his father was put back into poverty. By 1930, Woody was a high school dropout, painting signs, educating himself with frequent trips to the library, and beginning his serious interest in music. He took being poor and near homeless as a matter of fact, but he was resilient. Woody was shaped by the misfortune and unpredictability of his formative years and yet bravely accepted his lot. When his sister Clara died so tragically, he refused to cry. Instead, bearing such pain, he would become the clown, perhaps deflecting serious emotions with humor and lightheartedness. Whatever the case, Woody Guthrie was primarily fending for himself at an early age.

Then came the dust.

———————————————————

Just as the late 1920s oil boom was ending and the Great Depression was setting in, signs of drought were surfacing on the southern Great Plains. It turned out to be a drought of biblical proportions, one that lasted ten years and turned the place Woody lived into a region known generally as the Dust Bowl.

The dust storms that plagued huge swaths of the Great Plains in the 1930s were a man-made phenomenon caused by bad farming practices on land unsuitable for crop production.

A land that for centuries was a natural sod and grazing area for bison, and later for cattle ranching, was called a "no-man's-land" for a reason. Many generations of locals knew it wasn't a place to plant, due to the inconsistent rain and historic periods of drought. But unwisely, it was converted to large wheat farms during the successive land rushes that Guthrie's family was a small part of.

Land misuse got even worse after Charley Guthrie was forced out of the market. In the 1920s, new, industrial-style farming with mechanized equipment and motorized tractors with doubly effective plows encouraged landowners to buy more and more land in order to plant more and more wheat. Farmers added headlights to their tractors so they could plow ancient sod all night. Easy short-term economic gain motivated "suitcase farmers" and real estate speculators to plant still more wheat and turn over still more land.

Compounding the problem was the government's decision in the 1920s to enlarge the Homestead Act and encourage more settlement in the southern Great Plains. It was an opportunity for first-time buyers to get a little piece of their own.

There was rampant fraud as land speculators tried to convince families to buy. Historian Ken Burns notes that the real estate hawkers told poorly educated buyers that the weather had permanently changed, that Oklahoma now had a wet climate. They even suggested that the "rain follows the plow, meaning the very act of turning over the soil would bring more rain."

For a while, in the late '20s, the rain did fall and goings were good. Small farmers prospered, and corporate farmers prospered even more, all of which resulted in more and more land speculation. But when the

Black Sunday dust storm, Pampa, Texas, 1935

rains stopped in 1932, farmers were left with nothing but dry, sandy soil that—on account of the wide destruction of natural grasses that once held it in place—was left to the whims of violent prairie winds.

There were thirty-eight dust storms in 1933. The scariest were the black blizzards that looked like a mountain range one hundred feet high. Burns notes that one storm moved more dirt in twenty-four hours than was moved during the entire excavation of the Panama Canal.

Guthrie was in the middle of it all. He later insisted that while the region known as the Dust Bowl often is associated with Oklahoma, "the blackest, the thickest" dust in the country could be found in the panhandle of Texas. He recalled for Alan Lomax the worst storm to hit Pampa—the Black Sunday storm on Palm Sunday, April 14, 1935.

"We watched the dust storm come up like the Red Sea closing in on the Israeli children," he said in his characteristic drawl. "It got so black when it came, we all went into the house and all the neighbors congregated. It got so dark you couldn't see your hand in front of your face."

People were losing hope. People were scared. Many thought the world was literally coming to an end—the apocalypse brought on by their sinful ways.

As Guthrie watched families stream out of Pampa in search of a new life, he wrote one of his first songs, a ballad that deftly captured the gallows humor of his weary people.

So long, it's been good to know yuh
This dusty old dust is a-gettin' my home

Looking back with today's perspective, it's almost unimaginable that such a disastrous convergence of dust and economic depression— two man-made problems—could occur. It was devastating.

Two hundred fifty thousand families fled. Many were victims of circumstance and, to a great extent, a faulty financial system. Woody was then twenty-two years old, and the Dust Bowl would be forever linked to his legend.

———————

It was in Pampa that Guthrie first became what you could call a professional musician, joining up with a group called the Corn Cob Trio and playing hillbilly music for dances and gatherings all over the region. He also freelanced as a musician for other groups, including a cowboy outfit that the local chamber of commerce put together. In 1933, Woody married Mary Jennings, the sister of his bandmate Matt, in the local Catholic church.

Despite the dust and the Depression, it seemed to be a comfortable existence for Woody Guthrie. He was playing music, had a strong social circle, and was close to family. He kept exploring books in the local library that grabbed his interest, took up yoga, and put together his first songbook in 1935; also that year, he and Mary had their first child, Gwen. While some folks had fled to California in search of a better life, they were able to get by on Woody's work as a sign painter and soda jerk.

But as the decade wore on, Woody's restlessness was getting to him, and he began looking to get out. At first he made small trips around the area, leaving Mary and their young daughter at home. He started talking about moving to California, which drew groans from family members who'd heard the poor fortunes that had met others when they'd left for that supposed promised land. He made his big move in the spring of 1937—without wife and daughter—when he hopped a freight train to California. After traveling up and down the state a little bit, he settled in Glendale with his aunt.

It was in Glendale that he teamed up with his cousin Jack Guthrie, a musical pairing that set the course for Woody's career.

Jack Guthrie wanted to be another Gene Autry. Cowboy acts were all the rage in California, and Jack thought that he and Woody made a good combination for a twangy show. However, most radio stations already had their own cowboy performers on air. One exception was the radio station KFVD, which was run by a populist named J. Frank Burke. KFVD was largely a political radio station, championing various liberal causes affecting California.

The two Guthrie cousins—content to sing the old songs of Oklahoma—were meant to be a break from political programming. But for Woody, the opposite was true: the station turned him political.

Jack and Woody were good enough to gain listeners, but they didn't make a lot of money. Like Woody, Jack had a wife and kids. Unlike Woody, he worried about providing for them, and after a few months

Woody Guthrie and Lefty Lou with sign for show on KFVD Radio in Los Angeles, circa 1937

on KFVD, he quit the program for more gainful work. Woody stayed on, and brought on a sidekick: Maxine Crissman, a.k.a. Lefty Lou.

The show *Here Comes Woody and Lefty Lou* was Woody's first exposure to wide popularity. The next two years proved beyond a doubt that Woody Guthrie had the charisma that could connect him to an audience. With Lefty Lou, he first started performing his own songs on the radio, many of which resonated with the listeners. Among them was the song "Oklahoma Hills," a tune that endures as one of Woody's most popular.

So many listeners wrote in asking for his lyrics that he began mimeographing songbooks in the KFVD office to sell to them.

Guthrie was apolitical when he arrived in Los Angeles, but working at the populist KFVD made exposure to leftist politics nearly inevitable; the ideology's focus on the working class was instantly attractive to him, and he quickly emerged as a political thinker in Los Angeles.

A Dust Bowl migrant himself, it didn't take long for him to see the deplorable way dispossessed farmers from the Great Plains were being treated. Fruit-farm owners had distributed handbills all across the Dust Bowl telling folks that good jobs and high wages awaited them in California, but that turned out to be just part of an effort to drive down labor costs for fruit pickers.

"They'd heard about the land of California, where you sleep outdoors, and you work all day in the big fruit orchards and make enough to live on and get by on and live decent on and work hard and work honest," Guthrie recalled. "And, according to these handbills passed out, you're supposed to have a wonderful chance to succeed in California."

When the flood of migrants came in response, many ended up as vagrants, which brought on the wrath of local authorities, who saw them as a scourge on their communities. It was common practice for state troopers to arrest people for being out of work, and then force them to work for free picking the fields.

"When you came to that country, they found different ways to put that [vagrancy] charge on you to get you working for free, either in a pea patch or a garden or hay or something, and so you were always working and you weren't getting nothing out of it," Guthrie recalled.

His song "Do Re Mi" summed up the raw deal he saw his people getting in California:

> Oh, if you ain't got the do re mi, folks, you ain't got the do re mi,
> Why, you better go back to beautiful Texas, Oklahoma, Kansas,
> Georgia, Tennessee.

As biographer Ed Cray notes, the song is a direct rebuttal of singer Jimmie Rodgers's assertion that the water of California tasted "like cherry wine."

KFVD's station manager, Burke, saw Guthrie as a strong new voice in the progressive causes he championed—among them, rights

Woody Guthrie and Fred Ross, manager of Shafter Farm Workers Community, California, 1941

for migrant farmers. Along with keeping him on the air—giving him a platform to play his new ballads—Burke hired Woody on as a "hobo correspondent" for his leftist newspaper, the *Light*. Guthrie spent time on the railcars and under the bridges to report on the economic plight afflicting his people. He also visited the labor camps set up by the orchard owners, where workers lived in squalor as they barely scraped by with their earnings from long days of manual labor.

Guthrie also visited the camps the Farm Security Administration established to give sanitary shelter to the migrant farmers—the same camps that provided John Steinbeck with his material for *The Grapes of Wrath*. Steinbeck and Guthrie met each other at this time, becoming fast admirers of each other's work.

The migrant worker camps—established by the Roosevelt administration to ease the plight of the Dust Bowl refugees—served as an important prologue to Guthrie's experience in the Pacific Northwest. Namely, they suggested to him that federal government intervention could improve the lot of the common man. The FSA built fifteen sanitary camps and, in the view of many, offered a dignity that had been lost in the depth of the Depression. As historian Richard Nate notes, Steinbeck's character Tom Joad mirrors Guthrie's own view on how the people could be helped with New Deal policies:

I been thinkin' how it was in that gov'ment camp, how our folks took care a theirselves, an' if they was a fight they fixed it theirself; an' they wasn't no cops wagglin' their guns, but they was better order than them cops ever give. I been a-wonderin' why we can't do that all over.

The Columbia River projects may have been the closest New Dealers ever got to "doing that all over," and Guthrie proved very excited by that prospect.

Burke also introduced Guthrie to several avowed communists who quickly became close collaborators. The two most important in Woody's life were Ed Robbin and Will Geer. Geer was an actor working under Orson Welles in a federal theater production—best known later as the grandfather in the TV series *The Waltons*. Geer and Guthrie traveled to migrant camps together. In fact, it

A Farm Security Administration migrant camp in El Rio, California, 1941

was Geer who first exposed Guthrie to the plight of migrant farmers. Meanwhile, Robbin hosted a political radio show on KFVD and was the California correspondent for the Communist Party newspaper, the *People's Daily World*. Robbin invited Woody to his first Communist Party event in 1939, a rally at which Woody sang and was a hit with the crowd. He also helped Woody get a column with the *People's Daily World*, called Woody Sez. The column—which typically ran about five paragraphs and sometimes included small drawings—displayed how fully Guthrie had developed his folksy take on politics in his few short years in Los Angeles. In a typical column published in 1939, Guthrie rewrote the Pledge

*Guthrie visiting
Shafter's camp in
California*

of Allegiance to read: "We pledge allegiance to our flag . . . and to Wall Street for which it stands . . . one dollar, ungettable."

Guthrie was certainly sympathetic to many communistic causes, especially as far as they would empower the poor workers in California. However, he was never a party man, and he always held on to a heavy dose of his Oklahoma Christianity when interpreting the world around him. Biographer Ed Cray described his patchwork of ideas and moral beliefs as "Christian socialism."

In his journal, Woody summed up his politics this way: "When there shall be no want among you, because you'll own everything in common. When the rich will give their goods into the poor. I believe this way. This is the Christian way and it is already on a big part of the earth and it will come. To own everything in common. That's what the Bible says. Common means all of us. This is old 'Commonism.'"

But not being a party man didn't mean Guthrie couldn't be stubborn on some points.

In a display of how deeply into politics Guthrie was during his two years in Los Angeles, he got caught up in an ideological fight that broke out on the American left in 1939 when the Soviet Union reached a peace pact with Nazi Germany. Many leftists who saw communism as a strong bulwark against fascism were repulsed by the pact and fled the party. Guthrie stuck with the party, writing songs that argued that anything that kept Europe out of war was good for the common man, since he bore the brunt of armed conflict.

That viewpoint didn't sit right with Burke, and Guthrie lost his show, leaving him out of work in Los Angeles. But Geer by that time had moved to New York, and gave Guthrie an open invitation. Woody was soon off to New York.

So long, it's been good to know yuh.

Illustration from the Woody Sez series by Woody Guthrie, 1939

BALLAD OF THE GREAT GRAND COULEE
(By Woody Guthrie)

✓ composed by W.G.

Well, the world has Seven Wonders, that the Travelers always tell,
Some Gardens and some Towers, I guess you know them well;
But now the Greatest Wonder's in Uncle Sam's fair Land,
It's the King Columbia River and the Big Grand Coulee Dam!

She heads up the Canadian Mountains where the rippling waters glide,
Comes a rumbling down the canyon just to meet the salty tide
Of the wide Pacific Ocean, where the sun sets in the West,
And the Big Bend Coulee country in the Land I love the best.

At the Umatilla Rapids, at The Dalles, and at Cascades,
Mighty men have cared a history of the sacrifices made,
In the thundering foaming waters of the big Celilo Falls,
In the Big Grand Coulee country that I love the best of all.

She winds down the granite canyon, and the bends across the lea,
Like a prancing dancing stallion down her seaway to the sea;
Cast your eyes upon the biggest thing yet built by human hands,
On the King Columbia River, it's the big Grand Coulee dam.

In the misty crystal glitter of that wild and windward spray,
Men have fought the pounding waters and have met a watery grave,
Yes, it tore their boats to splinters, but it gave men dreams to dream,
Of the day that Coulee Dam would cross that wild and wasted stream.

There at Bonneville on the River is a green and beautiful sight,
See the Bonneville Dam a rising in the sun so clear and white;
While the leaping salmon play along the ladder and the rocks,
There's a steamboat load of gasoline a whistling in the locks.

Uncle Sam he took the challenge in the year of thirty three,
For the Farmer and the Factory and for all of you and me,
He said, Roll Along Columbia, you can ramble to the Sea,
But River, while you're rambling, you can do some work for me.

Now in Washington and Oregon you hear the factories hum,
Making chrome and making manganese and light aluminum,
And the roaring flying fortress wings her way for Uncle Sam,
Spawned upon the King Columbia by the big Grand Coulee Dam.

                    From the collection of
                    Woody Guthrie,
                    Just migratin through.

CHAPTER 3

BALLAD OF THE GREAT GRAND COULEE

In the 1920s and 1930s, electricity wasn't just the stuff that made the light bulb work. For populists and reformers, it was a force to reshape society.

A good place to start in understanding that thought is the inauguration of Franklin D. Roosevelt as governor of New York on January 1, 1929. His inaugural remarks became a blueprint not only for his next four years in the governor's mansion but also, in many ways, for his years in the White House—especially pertaining to publicly owned electricity.

FDR's inaugural address to the people of New York remains to this day a strikingly progressive document, in which he lays out many of the themes that came to define him as president. It's an appeal to American society to abandon its rugged individualism for a new age of social cooperation.

"Our civilization cannot endure unless we, as individuals, realize our personal responsibility to and dependency on the rest of the world," he said. "The 'self-supporting' man or woman has become as extinct as the man of the stone age."

Nowhere did he see a better opportunity to realize this vision of public cooperation, he told the crowd, than on the rivers of New York, where he envisioned a system of dams producing cheap electricity for all the citizens of the state.

"In the brief time that I have been speaking to you, there has run to waste on their paths toward the sea, enough power from our rivers to have turned the wheels of a thousand factories, to have lit a million farmers' homes—power which nature has supplied us through the gift of God," he said.

Roosevelt considered any hydropower produced on the rivers of New York the possession of the people. And he believed it was his duty as governor to see to it that the power being turned into electricity was delivered to citizens at the lowest possible cost. He went on to outline his general views on transmission lines and power sites.

Went unsaid in Roosevelt's address was that at the start of 1929, a handful of powerful holding companies controlled the vast majority of America's power supply. By 1930, ten companies owned 75 percent of the electrical supply. Leading the companies was a who's who of American capitalism: John D. Rockefeller Jr., J. P. Morgan Jr., and Samuel Insull. State governments gave the companies charters, which granted exclusive access to power-generating stretches of rivers. But rarely did the companies act in the people's interest. In particular, the companies did a disservice to rural residents—those "million farmers" that Roosevelt referred to. Companies by and large had calculated how much it would cost to build transmission lines in sparsely populated areas and decided it didn't make business sense. This left huge swaths of America in the dark as electricity became a mainstay in urban areas. A United States Department of Agriculture study in 1925 found that of 6.3 million farms in the country, only 205,000 had electrical services.

For populist thinkers, it all added up to a raw deal. Private companies, given access to natural resources by the government, used them to selectively offer electricity to residents at a huge markup. In the '20s, progressives had started pressing for a new system in which the government oversaw the production and distribution of electricity itself to ensure that it benefited all citizens.

Indeed, that Roosevelt devoted nearly a fourth of his first speech as governor to hydropower demonstrates the populist hopes contained in hydroelectricity in the late 1920s.

"It is our power," Roosevelt said in his inaugural address. And "no inordinate profits" should be made from it.

By the time he was running for president three short years later, in 1932, Roosevelt had only grown more strident in his calls for the natural power created by rivers to be harnessed by the people for the people, rather than private corporations. Current events had made the public even more inclined to support his ideas. The stock market had crashed, the Great Depression had begun, and government investigations had found that private electric utilities had contributed to the economic collapse by fraudulently misrepresenting their earnings to inflate stock prices. A study by the Federal Trade Commission also found that private power companies had paid less in taxes than what they'd earned overcharging customers.

Roosevelt clearly thought it was time for his vision for New York rivers to be brought to scale on the national stage. On the stump in 1932, he

Harry Shaw's promotional piece for a WPA production called Power

FDR with Frank A. Banks, chief construction engineer of the Grand Coulee Dam, 1937

stopped in Gresham, Oregon, then in Portland, and laid out his ideas for a socialized power system that would get more electricity to more people.

Speaking to a crowd of eight thousand, Roosevelt said that electricity was no longer a luxury but "a definite necessity."

"It can relieve the drudgery of the housewife and lift the great burden off the shoulders of the hardworking farmer," he said. And yet he said Americans were "backward in the use of electricity," that even the Canadians were doing a better job—a statement sure to rile any red-blooded American.

It was time, Roosevelt said, to restack the deck and put citizens first with electrical power. Under his presidency, no utilities would gain private access to rivers, and power rates would drop.

"I have spoken on several occasions of a 'new deal' for the American people. I believe that the 'new deal,' as you and I know it, can be applied to a whole lot of things. It can be applied very definitely to the relationship between the electric utilities on the one side, and the consumer . . . on the other," he said.

The Columbia River makes its final, lumbering push to the Pacific Ocean not far from where Roosevelt proposed his new deal on energy. Whatever unrealized wealth Roosevelt had seen in the undammed rivers of New York State, the Columbia dwarfed it in magnitude.

By volume, the Columbia ranks as the fourth-largest river in North America. But its true might comes from the breakneck speed at which it carries that water from the northern Rocky Mountains to the sea. The river's drop of two feet per mile is almost four times greater than the Mississippi, an incredible source of power that in 1932 was still largely untapped. A study by the Federal Power Commission in the '30s estimated that the Columbia Basin contained 41.4 percent of all undeveloped hydroelectricity in the United States.

Many in the Pacific Northwest suspected that private utilities failed to develop the river on purpose so they could "corner the supply and hold up the price," as Seattle City Light superintendent J. D. Ross put it. It was deeply frustrating to the local farmers who—like farmers across the country—went underserved due to profit motives. Rural housewives were particularly galled, making them a major agent of change in the coming decade as they recognized that washboards were a thing of the past.

This rural agitation toward large private energy companies was expressed most forcefully through a farmers' organization that has long been the very manifestation of rural populism: the Grange. Founded in 1867, the National Grange of the Order of Patrons of Husbandry was conceived as a way farmers could come together to "learn and grow to their full potential as citizens and leaders." In modern terms, it's tempting to label Grange politics of the '20s and '30s as "liberal," but in truth

Ballad of the Great Grand Coulee

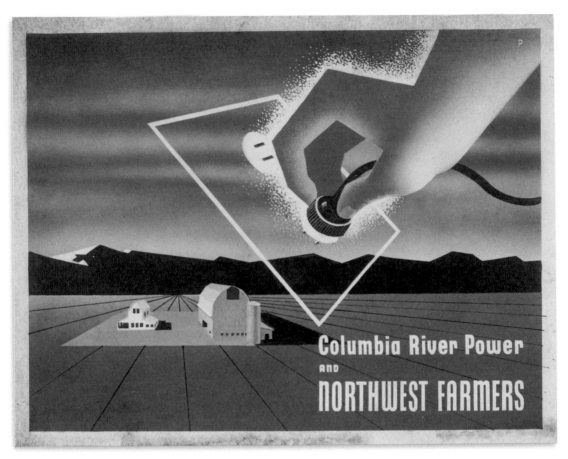

BPA poster illustrated by Lloyd Hoff, circa 1943

they defy any contemporary labels. Best put, the Grange was an organization that looked after the interests of small independent farmers, and more often than not, those interests were directly at odds with large corporations, including the power trusts.

Well before Roosevelt arrived in Portland, the Washington State Grange was mounting campaigns to establish publicly owned utilities to ensure that rural residents could get access to electricity at a reasonable rate. In a 1930 campaign to change Washington State law to allow for so-called "people's utility districts" (the "people's" being a populist spin on the more subdued "public utility districts" language actually used in the legislation), Grange Master Albert Goss employed the sort of lofty rhetoric that was commonplace in the fight for public power at the time. "The biggest trust of all time is the power trust," he said. "Its immediate aim is to lay hold of the water power of the nation and set the ever-falling streams to pour gold into its coffers."

If there could just be the political will to do so, people like Goss believed, the power of the Columbia River could be put into the hands of the people, not corporations, and sold at cost, not for gold going to company coffers; this big unharnessed engine of a million horses would be the catalyst for creating a new society, better technology, and the new infrastructure in which to build a "new promised land." And it would bring jobs.

In Gresham, Roosevelt was promising such a political will.

"The next great hydroelectric development to be undertaken by the federal government must be that on the Columbia River," he told the crowd.

Less than two months later, every state in the Columbia Basin — Washington, Oregon, Idaho, and Montana—voted for Roosevelt and his New Deal. And the New Deal wasn't long in taking shape.

Congress acted rapidly after the 1932 elections and authorized funds for construction of the Bonneville and Grand Coulee Dams under the National Industrial Recovery Act of 1933. By 1937, the

Looking for work at the Bonneville dam site

Bonneville Dam, forty miles up the Columbia from Portland, was producing power.

The sudden damming of the Columbia was an accomplishment in itself, but the Roosevelt administration wanted to go a step further. It wanted the federal government to sell the new power directly to customers—similar to what it had done in Appalachia with the Tennessee Valley Authority starting in 1933. Roosevelt's plan for the Columbia didn't sit right with many in the region, however, and just a month before Bonneville went live, a compromise was struck to create the Bonneville Power Administration. Put under the leadership of Ross,* a strong public-power advocate, the BPA created a

*J. D. Ross had a unique relationship with the Columbia River projects. As head of Seattle City Light and a catalyst for public power since the turn of the century, he was hand chosen by FDR to be the first administrator of the BPA. Both Ross and FDR advocated for the "postage stamp" plan, a system based upon charging customers uniform rates for power, regardless of their distance from the generating facility. Roosevelt secured his vision of the widest distribution of power at the cheapest possible price when Ross built his master grid in 1939—a region-wide network of transmission lines connecting both dam projects. Ross held both his city and federal jobs simultaneously but waived his salary for holding the federal post. He is buried at the site of his greatest achievement and the place he called home near the dam and lake that bears his name in the North Cascades.

transmission grid across the Pacific Northwest, from which it sold power to local utilities—preferably ones owned by the public. He died an untimely death in 1939 after undergoing abdominal surgery at the Mayo Clinic, so he never had the chance to meet the folksinger who put the populist dream of the Columbia River projects to song. But it was Ross who laid the groundwork for Woody Guthrie's experience in the Pacific Northwest.

J.D. Ross, first BPA administrator, 1938

Ross wasn't one to play the aloof bureaucrat, staying above the messy political debates over electricity. Rather, he spoke forcefully about the ways in which he envisioned people using power in the future—he rightly predicted Americans would soon be using a lot more of it—and insisted that the best way for people to light their homes was through a partnership between the federal BPA and local public utility districts (PUDs).

Ross hired Stephen Kahn to run public relations for the agency, and Kahn immediately became interested in how he could use film to make the case for public power.

From his vantage point in Portland, it wasn't hard for Kahn to see the benefits of public dams, no matter which way he looked. In the Hooverville at Sullivan's Gulch, Kahn saw real evidence of people who would benefit from cheap home electricity and better farm irrigation—a major byproduct of the dams. In Kahn's eyes, the huge projects on the Columbia River created a sense of tangible hope.

Stephen Kahn, left, the BPA's information officer

"The purpose of this whole development of the river is to raise the standard of living of the people here by giving them water and power and navigation and flood control," Kahn reasoned while surveying Portland's slums. He also saw the war industries flocking to the area, in part thanks to the availability of electricity, a strong economic force literally being powered by the government's harnessing of the mighty Columbia.

Kahn's first attempt to make the case for the BPA with film was a short documentary called *Hydro*, released in 1939, which he made with the help of producer Gunther von Fritsch. Running thirty-three minutes and scored with soaring orchestral music, *Hydro* was exactly the movie you'd expect to be produced by an agency of the Department of the Interior.

The movie was popular as far as it went. In 1944, Vice President Henry Wallace had the film translated into a half dozen languages for a tour of Asia, during which he pointed to the Columbia projects as an example of how democracy could be used to generate power for the people.

As displayed by *Hydro*, early in their efforts to promote PUDs, Bonneville officials were keen to make their case with technical and financial arguments. It's hard to blame them: the figures were on their side. Early adopters of PUDs saw cheaper power than those served by private corporations, and, as expected, they used more electricity.

Despite the low rates and technical prowess exalted by the BPA, it was clear that the region wasn't totally sold on public power at the close

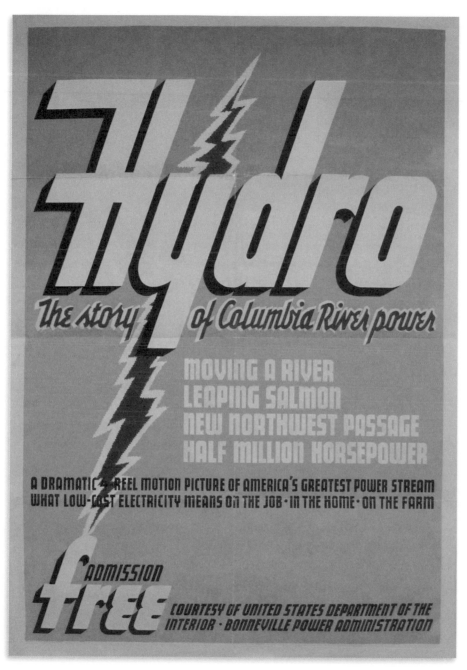

Poster for the BPA film, Hydro, *1939*

of the 1930s. In a major defeat for public power, voters in seven Oregon counties rejected a measure that would have created a large publicly owned utility company in 1938. The measure had come under heavy attack from private utility companies, and the election results showed that voters were still wary of the concept of the government becoming too heavily involved.

Immediately after the release of *Hydro*, Kahn was contemplating how he could make an even better film. He was not the only government employee using film to sell the New Deal, and he began talking to directors in Washington, DC, and New York City for guidance on how to create a successful political documentary. Among those he consulted was Pare Lorentz, who had worked on Great Depression documentaries. Dubbed FDR's filmmaker, Lorentz was instrumental in promoting the Tennessee Valley Authority's dam project and land reclamation in the 1937 documentary *The River*, which he wrote and directed for the Department of Agriculture. He had also produced the Dust Bowl classic *The Plow That Broke the Plains* in 1936.

Kahn came to believe that an effective film would not only relate the hard numbers of public power, but would capture the spirit of it as well.

"You have to have something that will introduce entertainment value and will go away lifting peoples' spirits and singing their songs," Kahn remembered thinking at the time. "You know, someone said, 'I don't care who writes your laws if I can sing your songs.'"

In other words, the Columbia River needed a song.

He himself tried his hand at writing some ballads about the Columbia and its power. The opening stanza of one of his songs went:

> *We face Columbia's fury from the Rockies to the sea*
> *And we brought to life the vision of a land that was to be,*
> *Of a land that men had dreamed of, from the Grecian days 'til now,*
> *Where true democracy is realized, can Columbia show us how?*

Transmission towers depict the power produced by the Grand Coulee Dam, Washington

© 1947 WESTERN SOUVENIRS 508

The Grand Coulee Dam with transmission lines carrying hydroelectricity

Those lines never found their way into the Great American Songbook, but they display the sort of romance Kahn hoped to infuse the BPA's staid rhetoric with. By 1940, work was underway to create the BPA's feature film—a movie that would make the most forceful sell yet on why people should want their government involved in the power business. Kahn put together a script that was good enough for superiors in Washington, DC, to allow him to move forward. Then he called on von Fritsch again to help him produce the film.

It would be called *The Columbia: America's Greatest Power Stream*, and it would capture once and for all the spirit and power of the Columbia River.

Now it just needed someone to sing its songs.

JACKHAMMER BLUES
(By Woody Guthrie)

Jackhammer John was a Jackhammer man,
Born with a jackhammer in his hand,
    Lord, Lord, and he had them Jackhammer Blues.
I built your roads, and buildings, too,
And I'm a gonna build a dam or two,

    Lord, Lord, well, I got them Jackhammer Blues.

I was borned in Portland Town,
Built ever port from Alasky down;
    Lord, Lord, well I got them Jackhammer Blues.
Built your bridges, dug your mines,
Been in jail a thousand times,
    Lord, Lord, well, I got them Jackhammer Blues.

Jackhammer, Jackhammer, where you been?
Been out a chasin' them gals again;
    Lord, Lord, well, I got them Jackhammer Blues;
Jackhammer Man from a Jackhammer Town,
I can hammer on a hammer till th' sun goes down,
    Lord, Lord, well, I got them Jackhammer Blues.

I hammered on th' Boulder, hammered on th' Butte,
Columbia River on a Five Mile Schute;
    Lord, Lord, well, I got them Jackhammer Blues;
Workin' on th' Bonneville, hammered all night,
A tryin' to bring the people some electric light;
    Lord, Lord, well, I got them Jackhammer Blues.

I hammered on Bonneville, Coulee, too,
Always broke when my job was through;
    Lord, Lord, well, I got them Jackhammer Blues;
I hammered on th' river from a sun to sun,
Fifteen million salmons run;
    Lord, Lord, well, I got them Jackhammer Blues.

I hammered in th' rain, I hammered in th' Dust,
I hammered in th' Best, an' I hammered in th' Worst;
    Lord, Lord, well, I got them Jackhammer Blues;
I got a Jackhammer Gal just sweet as pie,
And I'm a gonna hammer till th' day I die,
    Lord, Lord, well, I got them Jackhammer Blues!

        (I wrote my first Jackhammer Blues when I was a livin' in a
little old hotel up in New York Town, and the boys was a takin
up the pavement just below my window; but here it is set to a
little faster time, and out in one of the fastest, youngest,
hardest working countries you ever seen, in the rough and

tumble valley of the big Columbia River, out here in the good
old Pacific Northwest, Oregon.

                                    Woody Guthrie
                                    This song written May 12, 1941

CHAPTER 4

RAMBLIN' BLUES (NEW YORK TOWN)

When Woody Guthrie arrived in New York City in 1940, he called himself "The Dustiest of the Dust Bowlers."

It was an enticing moniker for the urbane crowd that had gathered at the Forrest Theatre at West Forty-Ninth Street on March 3 for "A 'Grapes of Wrath' Evening." While the devastating drought that was turning farmland to dust across the nation had been going on for ten years by then, Steinbeck's novel had renewed interest in the farmers' plight. The crowd knew that proceeds from the event would go to helping the dispossessed farmers thousands of miles away.

Now, here before them was a man who seemed to have been blown straight off the pages of Steinbeck's book, all the way across the Great Plains until he came to rest there on the stage, a guitar in his hand and homespun ballads on his lips.

The Woody Guthrie onstage at the Forrest Theatre was a folksinger in the purest sense, a character of the American vernacular. In the tradition he was faithfully carrying on, the term "singer" was used broadly, since the performer was likely to talk as much as he sang. What the slight and diminutive folksinger represented was a living piece of western folklore—a road-traveling Dust Bowler, just passing through.

But he was much more than a caricature of a dusty migrant. There was depth to his act. The mixing of message through ballads and stories

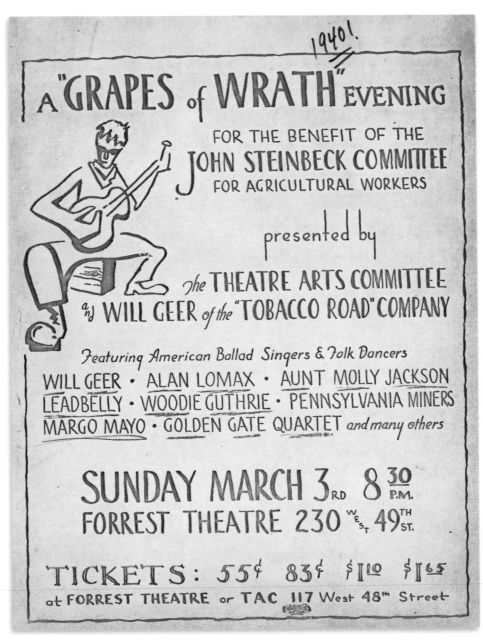

Flyer for Steinbeck benefit concert at the Forrest Theatre in New York City, 1940

was immediately memorable to the crowd—and he certainly knew how to put on a show. In that sense, what Woody was doing was "telling you something you already knew," which would be his calling card for many years to come.

He wore a five-gallon Stetson pressed down over his wild thatch of curly hair, a work shirt on his back, and blue jeans over his boots. He needed a shave but gave no hint of feeling out of place in front of the small crowd of well-heeled easterners.

Considering the regional nature of music and culture in 1940, to attend this concert and witness an unheard of "Okie" ballad maker from a faraway place must have been exotic, to say the least, for the New York crowd.

Of course, there was plenty of showmanship involved in Guthrie's stage presence—he had never worked on a farm; he had really never labored at all. Still, he knew what he was talking about, and he perfectly channeled the mood of the nation: down but not out, laughing to keep from crying. He told the crowd that he had relatives under every bridge in California and earned a good chuckle with his gee-whiz take on New York City.

"New York sure is a funny place," Guthrie drawled out at one point. "The buildings are so high the sun don't come out until one thirty in the afternoon, and then it's visible for seven minutes between the Empire State Building and the shoe sign over there."

"It was an act, obviously, but it felt so fantastically real," singer and composer Earl Robinson recalled of the performance.

When Woody got to singing, it was a combination of old cowboy songs from Oklahoma and Texas and new songs he'd written about the Dust Bowl and the plight of workers in California.

The crowd was enthralled.

"It was terribly understated," Robinson said. "It didn't look like much. But he made you look twice."

Also on the bill that night at the Forrest Theatre were a host of racially mixed singers and players who later came to have their own place as vital chroniclers of the American experience. There was Lead Belly, the Louisiana blues singer; Aunt Molly Jackson, just off the labor lines in Kentucky coal country; the gospel group the Golden Gate Quartet; and new blues singer Josh White.

And in Woody Guthrie, they had a Dust Bowl refugee, ready to regale them with stories of life at the very center of the American Great Depression.

In New York in 1940, there was widespread interest in folk music in the intellectual and academic scene. Political liberals and social progressives wanted to know more about this vernacular music from the invisible pockets of otherwise unpublicized places. The urbanites' world view was getting bigger as interest in rural traditional voices grew via the new documents of "the people's idiom"—in film, literature, photographs, and songs.

The Forrest Theatre concert was a demonstration of the oral tradition—that musical phenomenon in which songs have been transmitted from one generation to another for hundreds of years. From the Old World to the New World, traditional songs have traveled the so-called "carrying stream" to find new interpreters and new adaptations in a shared community over and over again.

Before radio and recording technology, songs were passed from person to person for many years until they were eventually written down. Song manuscripts were sold on street corners in old England as a way of telling the news, often as parody. These "broadsides" evolved into songbooks that popularized folk songs—often citing a known melody in which to sing. This is how people shared songs.

When new American immigrants settled in specific mountain valleys, rural stretches of plains, and southern plantations, the songs went with them and thus music became highly regionalized, both in style and subject matter. And this led naturally to adaptation as songs passed through the hands of successive generations. Like all stories, each person who touches it puts his or her own stamp on it. This has become known as the "folk process."

But by the 1930s, radio was having an effect on young performers. More and more talented musicians coming from the country seemed intent on styling themselves after Jimmie Rodgers, the yodeling cowboy singer, rather than people they grew up with. For not the last time in its history, folk music was considered at risk of becoming an academic exercise, something preserved only by oddball collectors, rather than a true reflection of the culture of the American working class.

Eastern academics and music collectors had thought the tradition was dying out in the 1930s, that authentic American voices could not survive the onset of mass media. Indeed, the federal government created an initiative to send archivists across the country to record regional music before it completely vanished. What they found, though, was an amazing wealth of vernacular music, representing real, unrecognized Americans in a variety of rural places.

Aunt Harriett at the microphone with John A. Lomax Sr. near Sumterville, Alabama

By the time Woody Guthrie took the stage in New York, fears that folk music would soon be completely dead had eased. Still, students

Will Geer's CBS promotional photo, 1940

of folk music were uneasy about the state of the people's music. Big bands, swing, and Hollywood cowboy singers were getting all the play.

The exoticness and uniqueness of the rural performers on the Forrest Theatre stage partly explains why a crowd had come out in the first place. They were hoping that their patronage could keep the folk tradition alive.

What was happening in New York was the emergence of a folk revival; it would fully blossom later, in the 1950s and early '60s, with a new generation of musicians who would find American vernacular music exotic and fresh. Just like the crowd at the Forrest Theatre that March evening, they were looking for the true unfiltered sound of real people.

The folk revival of the 1930s was heavily influenced by politics. Academics felt that folk music could imbue the working class with a pride that popular music could not, and raise broader awareness of the social injustice faced by poor people across the country. The labor movement, the preeminent liberal cause of the prewar years, was carried out to a soundtrack of folk songs.

Woody, no country rube, was keenly aware of the political weight music carried at the time, evidenced by a song he started in February 1940 while living in a run-down hotel near Times Square. With war seemingly on the horizon, there had been a revival of patriotic songs, among them Irving Berlin's 1918 anthem "God Bless America." Guthrie found the song to epitomize a conservative mind-set that turned

America into something sacred and not to be meddled with. Music should inspire people to take control of their lives, Guthrie thought, and demand what's rightfully theirs. Sitting there in New York, he wrote five stanzas to a song with the refrain "God blessed America for me." Only four years later did he change that line to "This land was made for you and me."

The concert at the Forrest Theatre had been organized by Guthrie's communist friend Will Geer, who was staging the benefit on a dark night of *Tobacco Road*, a play in which he was starring. The crowd was primarily influential leftist thinkers, fellow travelers, and those who saw folk music as expression for a new, reformed America.

And at the center of all this, and the ultimate spark for this folk revival, was Alan Lomax. His twenty-year-old intern at the Archive of American Folk Song, Pete Seeger,* also performed (a rather shaky version of "John Hardy").

Alan Lomax's publicity photo for Mutual Radio's Your Ballad Man, *1948*

*Pete Seeger was exposed to traditional music and folklore through the involvement of his father, Charles Seeger, with the Resettlement/Farm Security Administration's music projects in the 1930s, including folk festivals where he first heard the banjo. By 1939, he had dropped out of Harvard and taken a job in Washington, DC, assisting Alan Lomax at the Archive of American Folk Song at the Library of Congress. Seeger's job was to help Lomax sift through commercial "race" and "hillbilly" music, and select recordings that best represented American folk music. He has often been called the archive's first intern.

Alan, twenty-five, was the son of John Lomax, a former college professor who grew up in Texas and was one of the first archivists employed by the federal government; he is credited with discovering and publicizing the cowboy song "Home on the Range." Pete was the son of Charles Seeger, a musicologist and the person most credited for advancing the theory of folk process.

These two families, with their second-generation folklorist sons—enthusiasts, collectors, and players themselves—ultimately proved to be the figureheads of a movement that defined and shaped the popularity of folk music as a commercial genre in the twentieth century.

Along with other central figures like Moe Asch, the founder of Folkways Records, the pillars of a folk revival were in place when Woody came blowin' down that dusty road for his second-ever performance in New York City, onstage with the Martin guitar he'd indefinitely borrowed from Geer's wife.

By all accounts, Lomax's first experience hearing Woody Guthrie sing was nearly a religious one. His immediate impression was that Guthrie was a reincarnation of Will Rogers, the political humorist—also from Oklahoma—who'd died in a plane crash in Alaska five years earlier. Just like Rogers, Guthrie could spin simple yarns about simple folk, running his hand through his hair the whole time, and make it all sound profound.

But on a larger scale, Guthrie struck Lomax as the rare folksinger who was actually writing new ballads. For a miner of folk traditions like Lomax, Woody onstage represented a mother lode of material that Lomax felt he had to get on tape. Lomax seemed aware that Guthrie was in part an act. But he found him to be authentic enough. The ballads Guthrie was writing were good enough "to fool a folklore expert," he said.

Alan Lomax would have known. He was eighteen when his father was brought on by the Library of Congress as an archivist of folk music. John Lomax brought his son along on his first folksong-gathering expedition, during which they traveled across Texas collecting music. They visited farms, prisons, and small towns, asking people to share their music with the archive. That expedition was the first of countless for Alan Lomax, who in 1937 was officially hired by the federal government as the Archive of American Folk Song's assistant in charge and soon thereafter was recognized as the preeminent collector of American folk music. The Lomaxes eventually collected more than ten thousand sound recordings. Along with Lead Belly and Woody Guthrie, they recorded artists including Muddy Waters, Jelly Roll Morton, and Big Bill Broonzy.

Young as he was, Alan Lomax was already a strong-headed, opinionated, and forceful man. Henrietta Yurchenco, a fellow collector of folk music, described his personality in choice terms: "Alan had the most colossal ego I've ever seen in my life."

Needless to say, he wasn't shy about approaching Guthrie backstage after the Forrest Theatre concert. It would be wrong to say that the two couldn't be more different—Lomax had been born and raised in Texas, only later moving to Washington, DC, to work for the government. Still, the two men weren't exactly cut from the same cloth. In publicity photos from the time, Lomax appeared clean-cut in a suit, his black hair combed over with a neat part; Guthrie reveled in looking like he just got off the road. Lomax was forward to the point of being brash; Guthrie feigned shyness. Lomax prided himself on being an intellectual; Guthrie rarely admitted to reading a book (the key word being "admitted").

Lomax later recalled that Woody seemed a bit put off when he first introduced himself, that Woody was "somewhat skeptical" of the urbane folk enthusiast. But he managed to talk him into playing him a few more songs backstage—among them, a ballad he'd written about the outlaw Pretty Boy Floyd.

If Woody was an anachronism in his role as folk balladeer, Floyd was a throwback of another type, a Robin Hood criminal from the hard-hit Oklahoma farmlands. Floyd was a bank robber by trade, but he gained the sympathy of farmers by donating food to the poor and destroying mortgage documents in the banks he robbed, thus freeing countless families from their debts. Repeating the lore he heard in the Oklahoma countryside, Guthrie also contended that Floyd didn't rob nearly as many banks as he was accused of, that banks about to go bust anyway claimed Floyd had robbed them in order to have an excuse. Floyd was a classic folk hero—"Pretty Boy Floyd is sung about on more lips and more mouths, and thought better of in more hearts, and is all around more popular than any governor Oklahoma has ever had," Guthrie once said—and Woody Guthrie was Floyd's troubadour.

If Lomax had any doubt about Guthrie's bona fides as a folksinger before hearing the ballad "Pretty Boy Floyd," he didn't any longer. As Guthrie biographer Ed Cray notes, the song to Lomax hit all the right notes; it was "a protest song," yet "a subtle, even sly protest song, that sprang from working class roots."

In Woody Guthrie, Lomax "found the kind of everyman he was looking for, who was a seasoned musician and also was close enough of the folk that he could pass for it," said Todd Harvey, curator of the Alan Lomax Collection at the American Folklife Center. "That was really good for Alan."

Lomax soon won Woody over, convincing him to be a guest on his national radio show and to record some of his songs for the Library of Congress archives.

A week later Woody was in Washington, DC, staying with Lomax and his wife.

Always the performer, Woody poured on his country-folk ways during that first visit to "Warshington," even at the Lomaxes' home. His hosts recalled that he ate over the sink and refused to sleep on a feather mattress—"I'm a road man. I don't want to get soft," he said. He also played folk records continuously and refused to take off his boots.

He was a tiresome houseguest, but Lomax didn't wane in his enthusiasm for the singer. Woody must have felt almost like a zoo animal as he was paraded around to other New Deal folklorists in Washington, including John Lomax, Benjamin Botkin, and Charles Seeger.

On March 21, 1940, Woody Guthrie sat down for his first recording session with Lomax in the Department of Interior's studios. They recorded for three days, and the collection represents the first professional* recordings of Woody Guthrie music.

Lomax styled his recordings as more of a chat with Woody Guthrie than a straightforward song-recording session. Says Nathan Salsburg, curator of the Alan Lomax archive, "Lomax frequently devoted space after performances during his field-recording sessions for brief interviews with the singers about where and how long ago they'd learned the song, who the source singer was, how long they played such and such instrument, etc. The Woody sessions were very much inspired by the long musical oral history sessions he'd conducted (previously) with Jelly Roll Morton and Aunt Molly Jackson."

The speaking interludes last longer than the songs, with Lomax practically gushing about the new friend he knew so little about, even his age. "Woody Guthrie is, I guess, about thirty years old from the looks of him, but he's seen more in those thirty years than most men see before they're seventy," Lomax says on the recordings. (Woody was actually twenty-seven.) "He hasn't sat in a warm house or a warm office. He's interested in looking out. He's gone into the world, and he's looked at the faces of hungry men and women."

*The Library of Congress recordings were eventually released commercially in 1967. Guthrie's first-ever recordings, however, were done at the radio station KFVD in Los Angeles in 1937 and 1939. These 78 rpm "air-checks" were recently discovered by Peter LaChapelle and are housed in Southern California's Library of Social Studies and Research.

The recordings are amazingly personal. With a tight throat, he shared that his sister had died after catching on fire, his mother had died in an insane asylum, and his father was severely burned in another mishap. Earlier in the session, Lomax had offhandedly said he wished he'd had the experiences Woody had had, so he could sing folk songs like him. This emotional interlude must have suggested to him otherwise: Woody's music was forged in a hot kiln of terrible hardship.

They wrapped up recording on March 27 and then headed back to New York. Woody's amazing run in the big city wasn't over—it had barely even started. On April 2, he was a guest on Lomax's educational radio show, *American School of the Air*, on CBS. He was paid $200 for that first appearance on national radio. On April 21, he was a guest on another national radio program, called *The Pursuit of Happiness*. In an introduction that slightly twisted the truth of Woody's origin, host Burgess Meredith told listeners that Woody was "one of those Okies who, dispossessed from their farms, journeyed in jalopies to California. . . . Not long ago, he set out for New York and rode the freights to get here."

Soon, Guthrie was the toast of many far-left American commentators, who saw him as the human manifestation of their homegrown socialist dream.

"Sing it, Woody, sing it! Karl Marx wrote it, and Lincoln said it, and Lenin did it. Sing it, Woody, and we'll all laugh together," wrote a columnist for the *People's Daily World*. Another wrote that Guthrie was "the most sparkling philosopher that ever hit the *Grapes of Wrath* trail."

Indeed, his identity was tightly intertwined with Steinbeck's work. And it was that April that Woody wrote the ballad "Tom Joad," which puts the story of *Grapes of Wrath* to verse and remains one of his most enduring songs. Even Steinbeck was an admirer. "That fuckin' little bastard, in seventeen verses he got the entire story of a thing that took me two years to write!" Steinbeck is said to have quipped about the song.

That same month, with the help of Lomax, Guthrie got a one-record contract with Victor Records, the company that cut the second recording of his life, resulting in his first commercial release called *Dust Bowl Ballads*. He got paid $400 or $300 (Woody wavered on the figure) and 5 percent royalties.

The record came out in July to critical praise but poor sales, the bane of countless other folksingers who followed Guthrie. Again, it was Guthrie's depiction of the hard-hit that caught the critics' attention. One critic said the album showed

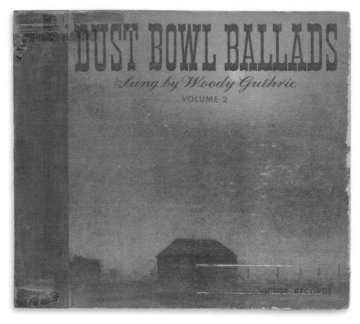

Dust Bowl Ballads *album cover, Victor Records, 1940*

"that life as some of our unfortunates know it can be mirrored on the glistening disks."

The poor sales were a drop of failure in a flash flood of success. Woody had taken a road trip down to Texas to see Mary and the children in June, and upon his return he was booked solid with performances. He was also getting on the radio more often. Radio producers weren't immune to the fever for folk music that was sweeping the city, and advertisers weren't ignorant of the sales potential that homespun performers could have for their products. Lomax, looking to move on from his educational programming to a more serious presentation of folk music, convinced CBS in August to try out a half-hour program he'd been developing called *Back Where I Come From*, and Woody was paid eighty-three dollars to be part of the pilot. CBS executives liked it enough to continue on, and Woody was signed on as a regular contributor.

Then came the ill-fated deal with Model Tobacco. From the distance of more than seventy-five years, it's easy to trace the fatal trajectory of

Woody Guthrie's first run in New York, as it tells such a common story of art versus commerce. But at the time, the money was just too good to pass up for the Guthrie family. Woody said the salary offered by Model "beats owning six farms in Oklahoma" and that he wasn't out to rock any boats with his newfound radio platform.

"It means so much not only to me but to my friends and relatives that I'll be able to help," he wrote Lomax after getting the deal. His wife and three kids were "feeling pretty good for the first time in a long time . . . down there in the dust bowl. . . . If I thought for two minutes that anything I do or say would hurt America and the people in it I would keep my face shut and catch the first freight out of the country."

Guthrie was referring to whispers that had been going around New York—mostly in letters to the editor responding to the positive press he'd been receiving—saying that he was anti-American on account of his politics. It was a prelude to the more serious red-baiting that would affect him, Lomax, and many others after World War II, but at the time it was more of an annoyance than anything else. Indeed, that someone like Guthrie, who had known associations with communists, could get a national radio program shows how much attitudes toward such matters had changed by the time the winds of the Cold War started to brew and Senator Joseph McCarthy entered the scene some eight years later. Still, it showed the pressure Guthrie was under to toe the line, even in the early '40s, if he wanted to make a living from his art. Ultimately, it wasn't saying something controversial but *not* saying anything that had Guthrie catching a proverbial freight train out of town, he and his family heading back West almost as quickly as they'd left.

For most of his run in New York, Mary and the kids had stayed in Pampa with relatives. But when he got the hosting gig, he sent Mary train fare and told them to make their way to the city. Woody rented an apartment and threw a party for his newly arrived wife that lasted days. Mary was suddenly wealthy enough to keep a few hundred dollars on her at all times.

26 SONGS *in* 30 DAYS

But the constant artistic oversight Guthrie was subjected to proved too much for him, and he quietly put in his notice at *Pipe Smoking Time*.

"He just walked away," his son Arlo—who wasn't born for another seven years—said of this chapter in his father's life. "I mean, here was a guy who had basically nothing, who was offered a nationwide radio broadcast, and as soon as he was told that he would have to write the kind of songs approved by other people, he was out of there like that."

The family's first stop was Washington, DC, where they visited the Lomaxes and Woody sat for a second recording session for the Library of Congress. Then it was on to Los Angeles for their ultimate winter of discontent.

It seems Woody had some remorse for his impulsive decision to split New York City just as things were going so well. Facing unemployment in Los Angeles, he wrote some letters to his old colleagues, sniffing around about getting his spot back on *Back Where I Come From*. But by that time CBS had apparently given up on its project of bringing authentic folk music to the airwaves.

Writing to Lomax from California in February 1941, Woody offered his condolences. He saw it as just another sign that no one really wanted to hear the truth about what Americans actually think.

"I'm sorry as hell to hear that Back Where I Come From is kicked off of the air," he wrote. "Too honest again I suppose? Maybe not purty enough. Oh well, this country's a getting to where it caint hear its own voice."

PASTURES OF PLENTY
(By Woody Guthrie)

comp. by
W. G.

It's a mighty hard row that my pore hands has howed,
And my pore feet has traveled a hot, dusty road;
Out of the Dust Bowl and westward we rolled,
And your deserts are hot, and your mountains they're cold.

I worked in your orchards of peaches and prunes,
And I slept on the ground 'neath the light of the moon;
I picked in your cotton, cut grapes from your vine,
And I set on your table your light sparkling wine.

We travel with the wind and the rain in our face,
our families migrating from place unto place;
We'll work in your beet fields till sundown tonight,
Travel 300 miles 'fore the morning gets light.

Arizona, California, we'll make all your crops,
It's northward to Oregon to gather your hops;
Strawberries, cherries, and apples the best,
In that sunshiny land call'd the Pacific Northwest.
It takes home loving mothers and strong hearted men;
Every state in this Union us migrants has been;
'Long the edge of your cities you'll see us, and then,
We've come with the Dust and we're gone in the Wind.

I picked up a rich clod of dirt in my hand,
I crumble it back into strong fertile land;
The greatest desire in this world that I know
is to work on my land where there's green things to grow.

I think of the Dust and the days that are gone,
And the day that's to come on a farm of our own;
One turn of the wheel and the waters will flow
'Cross the green growing field, down the hot thirsty row.

Look down in the canyon and there you will see
the Grand Coulee showers her blessings on me;
The lights for the city, for factory, and mill,
Green Pastures of Plenty from dry barren hills.

It's always we've rambled, that River and I,
It's here on her banks that I'll work till I die,
My land I'll defend with my Life if needs be;
'Cause my Pastures of Plenty must always be Free!

From the collection of
Woody Guthrie, Professional
Oakie, just a passin through.

CHAPTER 5

PASTURES OF PLENTY

A decade earlier, in the 1930s, America was trying to find its voice again.

In 1933, at the peak of national bankruptcy and four years after the stock market crash brought the economy to its knees, 12.8 million people were out of work—one-fourth of the entire working population. Gross domestic product nearly halved as factories and farms alike ground to a halt in the wake of Wall Street's devastation. The economic depression caused a crisis of authority in American society. Great financial institutions that had generated unimaginable wealth for certain segments of the population were now shown to be deeply flawed, and the government that was supposedly for and by the people seemed to have little power to help the suffering populace. The Great Depression was on.

From these ashes grew a new belief that the American economy could move forward only by relying on its underlying strength: the workingman.

To understand why Woody Guthrie was hired by the BPA in 1941, it is important to grasp the way in which folk artists like him had come to embody for much of the society both a look into the past and a path forward. By using the simple principles of common folks, people believed, America could reinvent itself as a populist utopia that was no longer beholden to private interests.

This was not an entirely organic phenomenon. A broad range of the American left—from New Deal Democrats to the Communist Party—sought to incorporate folk art into its vision for a reformed America in the 1930s. But while these organizations were embracing folk culture for their own purposes, the combined effect was a cultural renaissance. Among the work of this era stand some of the finest examples of Americana—not least of which are Guthrie's Columbia River songs.*

Franklin D. Roosevelt called them "the forgotten man." In a radio address in 1932 from the New York governor's mansion in Albany, FDR said that America's leaders had ignored the everyday worker in the economy. Instead, they'd put their trust in the "more spectacular" sections of the economy—namely banking.

"These unhappy times call for the building of plans that rest upon the forgotten, the unorganized but the indispensable units of economic power, for plans . . . that build from the bottom up and not from the top down, that put their faith once more in the forgotten man at the bottom of the economic pyramid," Roosevelt said.

When he was elected president nine months later, FDR didn't just remember the once-forgotten workingman. He made him the center of policies that sought to use workers—the farmer and the laborer—to claw the nation out of the depths of the Great Depression. In his first one hundred days in office, his government got fifteen major bills through Congress, affecting everything from banking—nine thousand

---

* Most all of the creative work produced by artists in the progressive communities of the 1930s embracing populism and the "people's idioms" are today considered classic examples of Americana. John Steinbeck, Charlie Chaplin, Lead Belly, Carl Sandburg, Orson Welles, Aaron Copland, and Frank Capra reimagined America in their work, while the new photojournalism of the Farm Security Administration created iconic images by Arthur Rothstein, Dorothea Lange, and Walker Evans, which were published in popular magazines of the time, "introducing America to Americans."

banks had failed—to agriculture, a sector of the economy that was seeing an average of twenty thousand farm foreclosures a month. Congress approved $500 million to shore up state welfare systems and launch public projects intended to put Americans to work.

In addition to a financial recovery, Roosevelt believed the hard-hit nation was in need of a psychological recovery as well. His reassuring "fireside chat" radio programs sought to soothe the fears of Americans enduring the worst domestic crisis since the Civil War. In the same vein, his government enacted policies that emphasized America's cultural wealth even as the economy struggled. In the words of historian Richard Nate, the Roosevelt administration explicitly attempted to "raise the people's self-confidence in a time of crisis." They did this in part by putting artists on the government dole who expressed the strength of the American character through telling the history of the common folk.

Overseen by the Treasury Department, the Public Works of Art Project hired thirty-six hundred artists to paint murals—many of which are still on display—in new public buildings in all forty-eight states. This initial program was disbanded in 1935 and replaced by an even more ambitious federal arts effort included in the New Deal's flagship Works Progress Administration.

The arts section of the WPA was called Federal Project No. 1, or Federal One. In the first year of its existence, the WPA allocated it $27 million—a significant amount of money but a small portion of the WPA's overall $4 billion budget.

There was some debate at the creation of Federal One about whether its main purpose was to simply give work to out-of-work artists or to explicitly advocate art that promoted an American version of progressive government. The latter was the assured result with the appointment of Holger Cahill as director of the Federal Art Project, part of Federal One. Cahill, a bit of a charlatan who greatly exaggerated his educational background, was a true crusader against stodgy classic art on the American continent. It was his belief that the best art is

WPA poster created by the Federal Art Project

that which is authentic to the place around it. As such, his objective was fostering new works that aimed to reflect the character of the worker's role in reshaping the American identity.

"Early on, he drew a connection between folk art, the art of everyday life, and the Federal Art Project," art historian Susan Noyes Platt wrote about Cahill's approach. She said Cahill shared the principles of museum director John Cotton Dana, who wrote that to study American art "is not to read works on esthetics or on the history of art production. . . . It is not to parade . . . through the art galleries of Europe." Rather, it was "to learn to know and feel this beauty in every-day objects which have been produced in America."

Cahill believed that by fostering American art for Americans, the government could help give voice to those who had once not had a platform in the United States and make the humanities more accessible to the masses.

"No great art has come out of schools and colleges of art, but out of centers like this," Cahill said in 1938 when dedicating an art center in Harlem that hosted black artists. "We are not particularly interested in developing what is known as art appreciation. We are interested in raising a generation . . . sensitive to their visual environment and capable of helping to improve it."

Cahill's anti-academic rhetoric, however heavy-handed, illustrated the convergence of public policy and art theory in the 1930s. The New Deal arts ethos could be summed up as one that celebrated the common man and favored dignity over destitution. A prime example of the government's efforts is found in the Farm Security Administration's photojournalism program. Photographers Dorothea Lange, Walker Evans, Arthur Rothstein, and others captured images that came to represent both the hardships of the times and the resilience of the people living through them. They sought to not just inform the public about the state of America but to move them.

Dorothea Lange
in the field, 1936

Many left-wing artists were stimulated by a new-found patriotism. Once shown the scenes and stories of their own country, it's as if they discovered their own culture—native and indigenous art forms and folklore never before broadcast to a wide audience.

John Steinbeck's *The Grapes of Wrath* and other defining masterpieces of the decade, such as Frank Capra's *Mr. Smith Goes to Washington* and Carl Sandburg's book-length poem *The People, Yes,* also reflected the cultural sentiment of the times.

In 1935, the Communist Party made a concerted effort to use folk art as a way to Americanize and make itself less foreign. Long a simple facsimile of European communism, the party in America came to understand that an atheist, militant movement would never gain a wide following in the United States. To soften its image and broaden its membership, in the mid-1930s, it began sponsoring a movement that came to be known collectively as the Popular Front.

As defined by historian Michael Kazin, the Popular Front was a "vigorously democratic and multiracial movement in the arts and daily life that was sponsored but not controlled by the Communist Party." The party sought to become less sectarian and to build coalitions with other like-minded American leftist organizations, ones that were anti-fascist and proworker. Suddenly, the Communist Party in the United

States stopped deriding FDR and the New Deal and became aligned with its goals of improving conditions for the American worker in the United States.

The party began espousing slogans such as "Communism is twentieth-century Americanism" and embracing art forms that it once despised—namely, popular film. With this softened image, it made successful entreaties to Hollywood, which soon flocked to the Popular Front. Americans who believed in everything from women's rights to racial equality were suddenly attracted to the broad coalition the Popular Front was building under the banner of the traditional American ideals of hard work and strong community. It's important to be clear that not all artists who were labeled "Popular Front" were communists. On the contrary, many progressive thinkers shared a cultural path with the Popular Front unified under the ideas of reform, the civil rights of all Americans, and, most importantly, taking a stand against rising fascism in Europe.

Historian Leonard Quart noted that the Popular Front seemed the "perfect embodiment of left-wing ideals" for Hollywood liberals. "For the first time . . . a large number of artists and intellectuals had found that through the Popular Front they could simultaneously belong to a 'radical' mass movement and be good Americans." Historians agree that the rise of the Popular Front heavily influenced American art in the 1930s, as it brought artists from a wide swath of American life together in a shared mission of creating works that celebrated the working class. It also helped the Communist Party for a time. During the Popular Front movement, the party saw its highest membership in America ever, reaching one hundred thousand. But the communists seemed to almost be a victim of their own success, as the music created by Popular Front artists was entirely incorporated into American culture—divorced from its intended communistic overtones (if any existed to begin with). For example, Popular Front member Earl Robinson's "Ballad for Americans" was performed at the Republican National Convention in 1940.

Just how closely these "fellow travelers" hewed to party-line Communism in the 1930s would eventually be the subject of congressional hearings. But at the time, it was not a pressing concern and there was fluid movement of personnel between the Popular Front and FDR's New Deal arts programs—both of which emphasized the same vague idea of exalting the common man by way of advancing a political agenda that promoted a new social democracy.

Whether you call it public relations or propaganda, much of the art created under Federal One and other government arts programs of the time often used the folk aesthetic lauded by Cahill to expressly promote federal programs—including public power and dams.

———————

The ultimate precursor to Woody Guthrie's entry into the Pacific Northwest was a play called *Power*. In 1937, the WPA's Federal Theatre Project debuted the play, which amounted to a folk-themed stage production that sought to get the public behind the idea of government-owned power by telling the story of the Tennessee Valley Authority. It was part of the Federal Theatre Project's Living Newspaper series, which put the current affairs of the nation on the stage through dramatic productions.

With the debate just ramping up in the Pacific Northwest, public-power advocates staged the play at the Metropolitan Theatre in downtown Seattle. Their partisans filled the seats of the playhouse, and publicly owned Seattle City Light donated large transformers to the theater to help set the stage. It was widely derided by conservatives for its folky tone and overbearing message. "That Old Debbil, the Power Trust, is the villain and the TVA is the hero in as fine a piece of overdone propaganda as ever trod the boards," the *Seattle Daily Times* sniffed when the production hit the theater. "The play has the subtlety of a sledgehammer and the restraint of a groundswell."

Poster of Seattle's production of Power, 1939

The Roosevelt administration was unapologetic for its use of federal dollars to promote its policies. In defending *Power*, an administrator gave a clear look at the sort of populist righteousness New Deal Democrats carried.

"People will say it's propaganda," WPA director Harry Hopkins told the cast following the first production of *Power*. "Well, I say what of it? If it's propaganda to educate the consumer who's paying for power, it's about time someone had some propaganda for him. The big power companies have spent millions on propaganda for the utilities. It's about time that the consumer had a mouthpiece. I say more plays like *Power* and more power to you."

Notable in the production of *Power* was its incorporation of folk music commissioned specifically for the play.

Years before the BPA hired Woody Guthrie to write songs about the Columbia River, the WPA commissioned a folksinger named Jean Thomas to write a song called the "Ballad of the TVA." Thomas is best known as the founder of the American Folk Song Festival, one of the first attempts in the country to formalize the "singin' gatherings" that were common in her home state of Kentucky. Thomas lacked the gift of subtlety that Guthrie would employ in his pro-public-power songs, but that fact makes her ode to the TVA a perfect example of the high-rhetoric optimism with which New Dealers hoped to infect the public, and the way they wrapped it in folksy packaging. At the end of *Power*, the actors took the stage, locked arms, and rejoiced, singing the TVA song:

> *All up and down the valley, they heard the glad alarm;*
> *The Government means business, it's working like a charm.*
> *Oh, see them boys a-comin', their Government they trust,*
> *Just hear their hammers ringin', they'll build that dam or bust!*

If the Tennessee Valley Authority was the test case in FDR's grand new public-works concept, then the Columbia Basin proved to be the next case. It showed what the government was willing to do to remake America, but on a much grander scale.

What New Dealers had in mind for the Columbia Basin would take the sort of planned farming communities seen in California to a scale that challenged credulity. Their solution to the Dust Bowl crisis and the thousands of displaced migrant families was a land reclamation project in the Pacific Northwest with newly irrigated acreage the size of Delaware dedicated to family farms. It was dubbed a "promised land," and that was just the start of the lofty rhetoric to come from the idea of harnessing the immense potential of a wild river.

New Dealers knew that a big dream like this wouldn't succeed without high-minded optimism and the support of the public, but the idea gained significant traction because Woody Guthrie and many others believed in it. For Woody, it was "what man could do" for his people.

The result was the Grand Coulee Dam, although it came with a high toll in human and environmental costs.

Over the course of a weekend in June 1940, Native Americans from across the Pacific Northwest gathered in Kettle Falls, Washington, for a three-day "Ceremony of Tears."

For thousands of years, the tribes of the Pacific Northwest were sustained by the salmon runs of the Columbia River. Salmon are anadromous fish, meaning that they spend most of their lives in saltwater but swim, or "run," up freshwater streams to lay eggs and die. With its wide mouth and passable waterfalls, the Columbia River was a vital highway between the Pacific Ocean and freshwater spawning streams from Oregon to northern British Columbia. Kettle Falls, located on the river just thirty miles from the Canadian border, was long a symbol to native peoples of the great bounty provided by the Columbia. They called the area "Roaring Waters" or "Keep Sounding Water," and as many as fourteen tribes traditionally congregated there during salmon runs in order to fish and trade. It was an ideal spot for fishing, as the eponymous waterfalls blocked the salmon's passage up the river, causing a mighty traffic jam of fish. There were so many, legend said a man could walk across the water on the backs of the writhing spawners.

But that June, tribal members knew that the falls, and the salmon, would soon be gone forever. The Grand Coulee Dam—the massive structure that Woody Guthrie would call the "mightiest thing man has ever done"—would soon be completed, backing up the river and creating a lake behind the dam, submerging the falls under ninety feet of water. Also submerged would be tracts of the Colville and Spokane Indian Reservations, requiring the relocation of more than twelve hundred graves. The salmon, meanwhile, already greatly impeded by the Bonneville Dam downriver, would be entirely cut off from a huge swath of their natural spawning ground. Within a few short weeks, the land that had sustained these people for thousands of years would be utterly transformed by an audacious feat of engineering that still stands today as one of the most ambitious—and, some argue, arrogant—in human history.

By today's thinking, it can be difficult to understand why a folksinger like Woody Guthrie, who proved willing to walk away from good money based on principles before, so vociferously endorsed a project like the Grand Coulee Dam. It killed salmon, took away tribal land, and powered war industries—all factors well understood by the time Guthrie arrived.

While some people have castigated Guthrie for his support of the dams, others have tried to apologize for him by suggesting he was naive and didn't understand what he was being asked to endorse. Neither point of view gets to the more complicated truth.

Guthrie was deeply affected by the collapse of the Oklahoma and Texas economies due to prolonged drought, and the limited options open to the dispossessed farmers who migrated to California. He was

The Grand Coulee dam backs up water forming Lake Roosevelt; diverted water is pumped uphill creating Banks Lake, a reservoir for the Columbia Basin irrigation project

also impressed by the efforts of the federal government to help migrant workers in Southern California—via the farm labor camps where he performed and Weedpatch Camp, which Steinbeck featured in *The Grapes of Wrath.*

To Woody Guthrie, the Dust Bowl balladeer, the dams were the answer to the ills of his time and the path forward for his people.

This fantastical and dramatic undertaking in the middle of nowhere began in earnest in 1933, but the story of Grand Coulee really begins thousands of years ago during the last ice age.

At that time, as massive glaciers began to melt on the American continent, cataclysmic floods repeatedly swept through an area stretching from present-day Missoula, Montana, to the Pacific Ocean. The floods were biblical in size—geologist J Harlen Bretz theorized that the flows contained five hundred cubic *miles* of water, ran six hundred feet deep, and lasted a month at a time. In the wake of the mammoth flows were huge dry canyons and channels called "coulees," carved by the huge volumes of water.

But even before the geology of the region was well understood, the idea of using dry river valleys and the natural tilt of the land for irrigation was percolating. Central Washington boosters understood that if you could just divert some of the Columbia River into the ancient Grand Coulee riverbed, gravity would turn it into a great irrigation ditch, stretching from the site of the current Grand Coulee Dam all the way to Pasco—hundreds of parched miles to the south. On account of the steep rock walls that line both sides of the Grand Coulee, the canyon could be turned into a giant reservoir to regulate the flow of the water. Making the idea all the more attractive was the fact that the farmland in the Columbia Basin—made up of rich loess soil deposited by ancient volcanoes—proved good for many early homesteaders, as long as it rained. If farmers could ensure that they got enough water every year, high yields were all but guaranteed. In this vision, the electricity produced by a dam was secondary. It would power the water

pumps needed to haul water out of the Columbia and into the Grand Coulee, and any surplus could be sold to pay for the construction of the rest of the irrigation system.

This crazy irrigation scheme was first dreamed up by some small town geniuses in Ephrata, Washington. Over lunch on a hot summer day in July 1918, a lawyer named Billy Clapp presented the idea to the visiting publisher of the *Wenatchee Daily World*, Rufus Woods. Woods and Clapp were part of an informal consortium of Central Washington businessmen intent on turning their region into an economic power-house, instead of the desolate stopover between Spokane and Seattle that it then was.

With the seed of a dam planted in Woods's brain, the idea now had a publishing platform from which to spread. Woods used his newspaper to highlight engineering studies that showed the Columbia River had 3.5 million horsepower of untapped energy and that the Columbia Basin contained 1.8 million acres of irrigable land. As historian Richard White notes, Woods presented the news not as dry engineering, but as a "melodrama" that pitted good-hearted workers in Central Washington against big moneyed interests back East.

From Woods's boosterism sprang a grassroots movement that saw farmers, industrial dreamers, and local advocates pressing for the Columbia to be harnessed for their benefit.

Over the 1920s, the idea simmered. Then in 1925 a US senator from Washington managed to get the Army Corps of Engineers to conduct a major study on the mechanics of a Columbia Basin reclamation project. While plan boosters focused on the irrigation potential for the dam project, the Corps focused in on the immense amount of power a dam would create. And it deemed such a project feasible. However, the report also noted that there was a big problem with damming the Columbia: not nearly enough people and industry in the region to justify all that electricity. The Corps concluded that it would sign off on dams built by private or municipal utilities along the river, but the federal government wouldn't be involved in construction.

Richard White suggests that had the 1930s been a normal decade, that report would have put an end to the idea of a dam at the mouth of the Grand Coulee. But the '30s were a time of upheaval, a decade of social transformation caused by economic destruction. With a quarter of adults out of work and public distrust of private interests at a peak, a massive public-works project along the Columbia River was precisely the kind of project Franklin D. Roosevelt had talked up during his run for president in 1932. Upon taking office in 1933, FDR almost immediately pushed legislation through Congress that approved the construction for the cornerstone of the Columbia River projects: the Grand Coulee Dam.

As with any major piece of policy, advocates for the dam didn't necessarily see eye to eye on specifics. To cite just one example, Rufus Woods was opposed to public ownership of electricity while his pro-dam ally, the Washington State Grange, was the driving force behind public utility districts.

But when the federal government took up the project in 1933, a clear vision for what the project would achieve emerged that was every bit as utopian as FDR's rhetoric on the campaign trail. With its alphabet soup of newly minted government agencies, the Roosevelt administration foresaw creating a new kind of agrarian society that, through engineering and government oversight, would be free of the turmoil that had plagued farmers since biblical times. Poor families with failing farms in the drought-stricken Midwest would have the opportunity to own newly irrigated land for cheap, the opportunity to start anew. Drought would be eliminated through irrigation from the river; overburdensome labor would be lightened by electricity; even the placement of townsites would be improved through careful planning. This was the "planned promised land," a term coined by historian Richard Lowitt to describe the New Dealers' vision.

Congress authorized a total of 2.5 million acres for the Columbia Basin Project. The number of acres projected to be irrigated by the project at its outset was 1.1 million.

Unlocking this much land for settlement inevitably led many writers at the time to hark back to the original expansion into the western frontier, which defined nineteenth-century America. Just as landless settlers had been able to forge a self-determined life through homesteading across the West via the Oregon Trail, so the newly landless Dust Bowl refugees would be able to do as well.

"I have heard these men talking about remote valleys no one has ever explored and secluded ranges no one has ever penetrated. . . . It is a frontier, and some day the country will spill the surplus population over in it," reporter Richard Neuberger wrote in his 1938 book, *Our Promised Land*.

The first step of conquering this frontier was building the Grand Coulee Dam. On November 1, 1933, the dam was named by the federal

Night scene of the Grand Coulee Dam under construction, 1939

administrator of public works as Public Works Project No. 9. It would span 4,173 feet at the crest and raise the Columbia River 550 feet above its lowest bedrock. The reservoir it created would run 150 miles, all the way to the Canadian border.

When construction on the giant dam began, it quickly captured the imagination of a nation. At a time when diversions from everyday life were a welcome respite, the story of "The Biggest Thing on Earth" was both a curiosity and a symbol of modern progress. Americans were infatuated with the movies, and Saturday matinees were standard entertainment in every town in the '30s. Typically a set of films was shown, including a feature, some shorts, a newsreel on current events, and public service announcements. Among items of national interest,

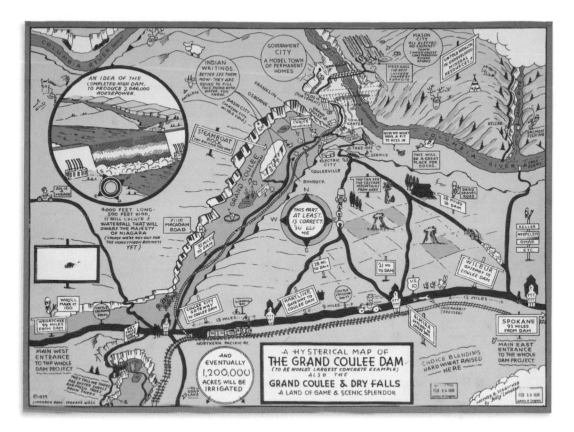

updates of Grand Coulee construction were regularly screened. Thus most every American, no matter where they lived, knew about the big project on the Columbia River in the middle of Washington State. And with the publicity came tourism. Soon curiosity seekers started making the trip to the desolate spot where the river bends to see for themselves the history in the making.

The small towns of Grand Coulee, Mason, and Electric City formed, and soon a small tourist economy developed, complete with postcards, tour brochures, comical maps called "hysterical maps," and other promotional items. The *Wenatchee Daily World* was a constant booster of the project, but the more conservative *Spokane Statesmen Review* also

Hysterical map of Grand Coulee by Lindgren Bros, 1935

Pastures of Plenty

B Street, Grand Coulee, 1940

ran copy of the goings-on in the desert. Something was happening, and all the hype was suggesting it was something big.

The Green Hut Cafe, perched next to the rising dam, was built to accommodate the tourists, the engineers, and their guests. The workers building the dam, meanwhile, could most likely be found during their off hours on nearby B Street, two blocks full of boomtown businesses catering to men, particularly bars and brothels. These establishments were open twenty-four hours year-round, in keeping with the around-the-clock schedules of work on the dam. The dirt stretch was hot, dusty, and dry in the summer and cold, muddy, and wet in the winter.

As large as the dam project was, though, planners believed it would soon be overshadowed by the even more ambitious irrigation project it was to feed.

Roosevelt envisioned an orderly relocation of farmers from across the country who would work small plots of land in the Columbia Basin. For every new acre of land planted, the administration hoped to take five acres of bad farmland prone to erosion out of production, thereby preventing another Dust Bowl. Conservative critics of the president thought his vision for the Columbia Basin verged dangerously toward a totalitarian agriculture program. Still, New Dealers were intent on using the power of the federal government to ensure that poor small farmers looking to start over would benefit.

Congress limited the size of farms irrigated by the Grand Coulee project to forty acres per farmer, and eighty acres for a married couple. To discourage speculators, aggressive controls were put on how much private landowners could charge for land in the Columbia Basin. Congress even gave the federal government the power to establish townsites there. Roosevelt saw the project as an opportunity not only to improve agriculture in the United States, but to actually encourage the development of an agrarian society over the urban one that would ultimately prevail in twentieth-century America.

"We will do everything in our power to encourage the building up of the smaller communities in the United States," Roosevelt said during a 1937 speech about the Columbia River projects. "Today many people are beginning to realize that there is inherent weakness in cities . . . and inherent strength in a wider geographical distribution of population."

These policies never came to full fruition. As such, it is difficult to understand how Roosevelt's vision would have played out in the Pacific Northwest. But suffice to say that under FDR, the federal government was intent on taking deliberate steps toward reshaping America as a carefully planned agrarian society. In the Northwest, that meant the federal government had established the infrastructure to deliver cheap irrigation to a network of small family-owned farms, what one New Dealer said would be a "modern rural community of a million people."

The "planned promised land" was all planned out.

Meanwhile, the power FDR had spoken of the federal government harnessing from the Columbia River was finally coming online. It was only five years prior that Roosevelt had visited nearby Portland and asserted that private utilities were overcharging customers and underserving the Pacific Northwest.

Appropriately, Roosevelt himself hit the switch at the Bonneville Dam that started the dam's two hydroelectric generators whirring on

September 28, 1937. He reiterated the populist thrust behind the project, noting not only the dam's power production but also the new system of locks that would allow large barges to ply the Columbia for the first time. "Truly," he said, "in the construction of this dam we have had our eyes on the future of the nation. Its costs will be returned to the people of the United States many times over in the improvement of navigation and transportation, the cheapening of electric power, and the distribution of this power to hundreds of small communities within a great radius."

With electricity flowing, the Bonneville Power Administration began building its transmission grid—drawing unsuccessful lawsuits from private utility companies that still hoped to keep the federal government out of the industry. And public utility districts, which connected customers to the BPA grid, were flourishing: between 1937 and 1941 alone, thirty-two PUDs were created in the Columbia Basin, adding to an already robust roster of publicly owned utilities in the region.

As promised, the system delivered drastically decreased power rates. BPA contracts between publicly owned utilities—be they municipal systems or PUDs—were reducing rates by an average of 50 percent. BPA administrator J. D. Ross expressly advocated for PUDs during local elections, and the BPA encouraged the creation of more PUDs by setting a policy of giving preference to public utilities over private and industrial ones. Roosevelt's Rural Electrification Administration provided these new utilities with cheap federally backed loans to allow them to build the infrastructure needed to tie into the Bonneville system.

The first community to receive power from the Bonneville Dam was Cascade Locks, Oregon. With a 3.4-mile transmission line between the dam and the town's municipal power system, the first public power started flowing in the Pacific Northwest in 1938.

The BPA wasn't just responsible for providing public power; it also was supposed to market it—which amounted to government-funded campaigns convincing people to use more electricity. Because of cheap

BPA poster advertising the consumer benefits of hydroelectricity, circa 1940

power, the BPA said in advertisements run in newspapers in the region, residents could embrace a modern lifestyle, with everything from electric coffeemakers to radios. "Forest Grove homes now can replace the old wood stove with a new electric range and their power bills won't be a penny higher than they were last year," read one advertisement for that Oregon community.

But while local customers were pleased, eastern observers remained dubious of the benefits of Roosevelt's shiny new public power program. They saw millions of tax dollars pouring into the projects for scant national gain. The dams at Bonneville and Grand Coulee were commonly referred to as "white elephants" and "boondoggles"—the epitome of New Deal excess. Those attacks ceased, however, as the prospect of war dawned on the nation.

As Hitler and the Japanese grew more bellicose in their actions, the United States began taking steps to supply its allies with war materials (and then, of course, troops). Back at Grand Coulee, as one observer put it, the dam itself was essentially "drafted" into the war just as it came of age.

Dam contractors rushed to complete the first power station there, and power began running off the dam in January 1941, two years ahead of schedule. By 1942, the dam was sating the hunger of aluminum plants across the Northwest. The aluminum was sent to shipyards, and to Boeing to produce planes like its "Flying Fortress," the B-17 bomber. Over the course of the war, Boeing produced 6,981 of the bombers in its Seattle plant. According to historian William Joe Simonds, in 1940 the Northwest had no aluminum-production capacity, but by the end of the war, it was producing a third of the nation's supply, nearly all on Grand Coulee juice.

In 1940, the BPA completed a 234-mile transmission line between the Bonneville and Grand Coulee Dams, creating the backbone to the system's grid, which still stands today. With power now running off both dams, the Columbia River had been harnessed. It was considered to be "the greatest system for hydroelectric power in the world."

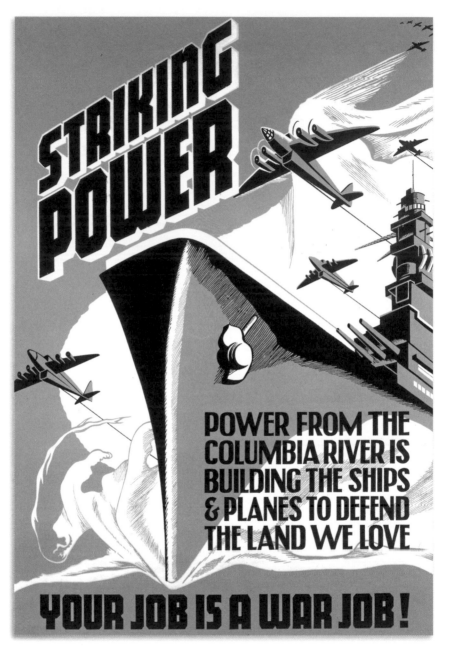

Cheap public rates, a new dawn for farming, industrial might with newly navigable waters, flood control, and ultimately the power needed to win a war—these were the great promises and future benefits that the Columbia River projects carried. But at the time of Woody Guthrie's trip to the area, the great costs were also understood: millions spent and billions yet to be spent on developing the irrigation system and increased power production; nearly half of all Columbia River spawning habitat cut off from salmon—more than one thousand miles of river and streams; and Native Americans losing their homes and traditional fishing grounds.

Still, for Woody, seen through the lens of war and Great Depression hardship, the benefits to the people were hard to pass up. The dam project was his idea of democratic socialism realized. It was what man could do to remake America and help people.

US Senator Homer Bone, Democrat of Washington, said as much when he addressed the tribal members gathered in 1940 for the Ceremony of Tears.

"We can build more airplanes and tanks and can train more pilots for national defense than any other nation or combination of nations, and the quicker we do it, the better. We know now that the only thing in this world that Hitler will respect is more force than he controls," Bone said. "The Indians have fished here for thousands of years. They love this spot above all others on their reservation because it is a source both of food and beauty. We should see to it that the electricity which the great dam at Grand Coulee produces shall be delivered to all the people without profit, so that the Indians of future generations, as well as the white men, will find the change made here a great benefit to the people."

Washington Talking Blues

Long about 1929
Owned a little farm, was a doin just fine;
Raised a little row crop, raised some wheat,
Sold it over at the county seat,
    Drawed the money. Raised a family.

But the Dust come along, and the price went down,
Didn't have the money when the bank come around;
Tumble weeds and the black dust blowed,
So we hit the trail to the land where the waters flowed.
    Way out across yonder somewheres.

Well, the hot old rocks and the desert sand
Made my mind run back to the dust bowl land,
But my hopes WAS HIGH AND WE ROLLED ALONG
TO THE COLUMBIA RIVER UP IN WASHINGTON,
    LOTS OF GOOD RAIN. LITTLE PIECE OF LAND. GROW SOMETHING.

WE SETTLED DOWN ON SOME CUT OVER LAND
PULLED UP BRUSH AND THE STUMPS BY HAND
HOT SUN BURNT UP MY FIRST CROP OF WHEAT
AND THE RIVER DOWN THE CANYON JUST 500 FEET.
    MIGHT AS WELL TO BEEN 50 MILES, COULDNT GET NO WATER.

WE LOADED OUR BELONGINGS AND WE LIT OUT FOR TOWN
SEEN THE OLD VACANT HOUSES AND FARMS ALL AROUND.
AND FOLKS A LEAVING OUT, IF YOU'RE ASKING ME
THAT'S AS LONESOME A SIGHT AS A FELLER CAN SEE,
    GOOD LAND, GROW ANYTHING YOU PLANT IF YOU CAN GET THE MOISTURE.

I STRUCK A LUMBER TOWN AND HEARD THE BIG SAW SING,
AND ~~I~~ WHEN BUSINESS IS GOOD, WHY LUMBER'S KING;
~~BUT THE SLUMP WAS ON~~ I WENT TO LOOKIN FOR A JOB BUT THE MAN SAID NO
SO WE HIT THE SKIDS ON THE OLD SKID ROW.
    TRAPSING UP AND DOWN. CHASING A BITE TO EAT. KIDS HUNGRY.

HEARD ABOUT A JOB, SO WE HIT THE WHEAT
MADE ABOUT ENOUGH FOR THE KIDS TO EAT,
PICKED IN THE BERRIES, GATHERED IN THE FRUIT,
HOPS, PEACHES, AND THE APPLES, TOO.
    SLEPT IN JUST ABOUT EVERYTHING EXCEPT A BED.

Been to Arizona, been to California, Too,
Found the people plenty but the jobs was few;
Well maybe its like the feller said,
when they aint enough work, well, business is dead,
    ailin. no money a changin hands, folks wastin gasoline a cussin around.

Now what we need is a great big dam
To throw a lot of water out acrost that land,
People could work and the stuff would grow
and you could wave goodbye to the old Skid Row.
    work hard. Raise all kinds of stuff. Kids, too.
        Take it easy.

                                    Woody Guthrie

CHAPTER 6

RAMBLIN' BLUES (PORTLAND TOWN)

Way back in 1940 or '41, I made a fast walking trip up and down the basin of the Columbia River and its tributaries, the Snake, the Hood, Willamette, Yakima and the Klickitat, making up little songs about what I seen. I made up 26 songs about the Bonneville Dam, Grand Coulee Dam, and the thunderous foamy waters of the rapids and cascades, the wild and windward water sprays from the high Ceilio [Celilo] Falls, and the folks living in thee little shack house just about a mile from the end of the line. The Department of Interior folks got ahold of me and took me into a clothes closet there at the Bonneville Power Administration house in Portland and melted my songs down onto records.

—WOODY GUTHRIE

Woody walked in wearing the khaki work shirt and matching work pants that he seemed to wear every day. He was bearded, unkempt, and reporting for a job that wasn't exactly his yet. It had been twelve days since the Bonneville Power Administration had sent him a letter stating that it was interested in hiring him to write songs for the agency and asking him to fill out paperwork to facilitate the hiring process. Instead, there he was, unannounced, holding a guitar and eating an apple, at the BPA

The 811 NE Oregon Street building in which Woody Guthrie worked; one of many BPA buildings in Portland at the time

headquarters at 811 NE Oregon Street in Portland, with his wife and three kids waiting outside in the car. The blue Pontiac was now in even worse shape than when it was used to haul firewood in the Sierra Nevadas. Guthrie had busted a window when he'd locked the keys inside, the upholstery was ripped, and the vehicle looked generally lived-in.

His hobo-beatnik style wasn't exactly what employees at the government agency were used to seeing. The BPA, just four years old at that point, was made up of engineers and bureaucrats. The only people who could have any use for a dusty folksinger were in the public information office, the head of which soon fetched Woody and shepherded him to his desk.

Stephen Kahn had heard of Woody Guthrie but had never heard his music, let alone met the man. He'd gotten his name from Alan Lomax, who had recommended Guthrie for Kahn's documentary project with a flow of superlatives over the phone from Washington, DC. "The idea that Woody would actually get a job writing ballads was just an inconceivable stroke, I felt like shouting over the telephone line, it was a laughing conversation all the way. I can remember the delight and (sense) of triumph I felt that Woody would get a chance to do this," Lomax recollected later.

The job Lomax recommended Guthrie for was a yearlong gig to be an actor, narrator, and singer in the documentary *The Columbia: America's Greatest Power Stream*. That was still the job description when Gunther von Fritsch visited Guthrie to take some photos in Los Angeles. And it was even the job description mentioned in the letter the BPA sent to Woody on the first of May—"Narrator-Actor, $3200 per annum." However, the May 1 letter also stated that the Department of Interior in Washington, DC, needed to approve the one-year contract. That, Kahn sensed from the start, could be a problem. The film's budget was tenuous, and war was looming. Then there was Woody's background. Even though Kahn was clearly a liberal himself and an activist for public power, hiring another activist who wrote columns for a communist newspaper, a known agitator and sometimes radical, was a whole other deal.

Ramblin' Blues (Portland Town)

Still, while Kahn hadn't officially offered Guthrie a job in the first place, now that he was standing in front of him, he didn't want to let an opportunity pass.

"He had his guitar, and I said, 'Play me something,'" Kahn recalled. "And I listened. And I said, 'Woody, I think you have the common touch.'"

The solution Kahn came up with right then and there was an emergency appointment, for one month. Such an appointment required approval only from within the agency, by the BPA's administrator, Paul Raver. Kahn set up an impromptu audition with the boss.

Raver had taken over the BPA shortly after J. D. Ross's untimely death in 1939. A gaunt, bespectacled former Northwest University professor, Raver wasn't the enthusiastic public-power advocate that Ross had been. He considered it inappropriate, for example, for the agency to get too involved in local PUD elections.

Perhaps anticipating Raver's conservative tendencies and fearing that Woody might start spouting ideology, Kahn gave the singer a warning. "Just play your guitar and sing your songs," he said. "If you talk, you'll lose the battle."

Woody sat on Raver's desk and did his best version of himself—"the man who told you something you already know" with the Will Rogers charm. He played songs for Raver and kept his talking to a minimum.

About thirty minutes later, Woody walked out with the job. An employment sheet calls him an "information consultant." His job description suggests that during his one-month employment, he would research the Columbia, study farmers' use of electricity, and determine the feasibility of creating a documentary and radio programs about it all. Only in the last sentence does it add "narrating and arrangement of musical accompaniment."

Guthrie later complained to friends that he had to fill out "five-feet of paperwork" when being hired on by the federal government. In that paperwork, which still exists in BPA archives, he wrote that he'd completed only through the eighth grade in school, that sign painting was one of his technical skills, and that he'd been unemployed since January.

The $3,200 annual salary listed for the original job was prorated, working out to $266.66 for the month he was there. Guthrie was disappointed at not having a full year's wages secured, but work was work.

And it would be work: one song for each day he was on the clock.

"I wanted to make sure that every day he produced," Kahn recalled. "Like in Hollywood, they require a scriptwriter to turn out three pages a day—or something, you know, no matter how good or bad it is. He had to bring in three pages."

Kahn told Woody he would be "over him with a stick" and require him to play the new music for him every day.

To prime Guthrie for the project, Kahn gave him three books: a history of Lewis and Clark, a history of the Columbia River, and a copy of *The Grapes of Wrath*, which Guthrie claimed to have not yet read.* Kahn also gave Guthrie a broad overview of PUDs, irrigation, and cheap electricity.

"He said, 'What kinda songs you want, Steve?'" Kahn recounted. "I said, 'Well, the purpose of the development of this river is to raise the standards of living for the people around here by giving them water and power and navigation and flood control and the whole bit.' He said, 'Geez, that's a big order.' I said, 'Well, that's why we got you.'

"Woody was thrilled with the prospect," Kahn continued, "and he saw it was more than a power or a reclamation or a navigation project

---

*In our research we discovered many, mostly oral, interviews of Stephen Kahn. In the videos and tapes dating back to the 1980s, he proves to be a man of high integrity and character, and we consider his memory of events forty-plus years prior reliable. He mentioned giving Guthrie a copy of *The Grapes of Wrath* upon hiring him to write songs for his film. Throughout our research it was hard to confirm whether Woody had read the 1939 book by May of 1941. He accepted the book from Kahn, and in a December 12, 1940, WNYC radio performance with Lead Belly, Woody introduces his new song "Tom Joad" by saying, "I didn't read the book, but then I seen the picture three times." The question is, did Guthrie deny reading the book in his determination to maintain his country rube persona? An interesting theory is suggested by BPA librarian Libby Burke; the combination of receiving the book from Kahn and driving those long road trips in the Columbia basin most likely resulted in Guthrie's writing of "Pastures of Plenty"—the ultimate song of the migrant experience with a promise of a better life in the new "promised land" that the Columbia waters could provide.

APPLICATION FOR EMPLOYMENT

RATED:

UNITED STATES
DEPARTMENT OF THE INTERIOR

Woodrow W. Guthrie
(Name)   112842

General Delivery
(R. F. D. or street address)   Personnel

Columbia   California
(City or post office)   (State)

Date May 12, 1941   Phone (a) _____   (b) _____
                        (Home)   (Business)

RECEIVED MAR 24 1941

1. Are you a citizen of the United States?	Place of birth: State or Territory. (Foreign-born citizens must prove citizenship. If naturalized, give name and location of court and certificate number.)	Date of birth (give month, day, and year)?	Age on LAST birthday?
Yes	Okemah, Oklahoma	July 14, 1912	28 years

2. In what State or Territory (or District of Columbia) have you legal or voting residence?	Length of such residence therein? (Residence must be shown up to date)	In what county have you legal or voting residence?	Length of such residence in county?
California	From Mar. 937 to Nov. 39	Los Angeles	From Mar. 937 to Nov. 39

3. Race White   Marital status Married   Sex Male

4. Are you physically sound? Yes   State any defects None

5. Height 5 feet 7 inches. Weight 125 pounds.

6. Are you now in the employ of the U. S. Government? (Answer "Yes" or "No") No If your answer is "Yes", state where and in what position and whether employment is permanent or temporary

7. (a) Were you ever employed in any branch of the U. S. Government? (Answer "Yes" or "No") No

(b) If employed, was your appointment permanent or temporary? —

(c) What civil service examinations have you passed?

(d) Are you eligible for reinstatement or transfer in accordance with Civil Service Regulations? —

(e) If ever employed, either permanently or temporarily, fill in the answers to the following questions concerning each period of your employment by the Government:

In what department or service were or are you employed?	In what city or town were or are you employed?	Dates of employment	Did you voluntarily resign?	Were you discharged?
		From ____, 1__ to ____, 1__		
		From ____, 1__ to ____, 1__		

8. Are you receiving an annuity from the Federal Government under the retirement act? No

9. (a) Are any members of your family or relatives (either by blood or by marriage) in any part of the U. S. Government service whatsoever? (Answer "Yes" or "No") No If so, furnish the information required below in regard to all such relatives:

Name	Post office address	Position and department or office in which employed	Relationship	Married or single
	Street and No. ____ City or town ____	Position ____ Department or office ____		
	Street and No. ____ City or town ____	Position ____ Department or office ____		
	Street and No. ____ City or town ____	Position ____ Department or office ____		

(b) Does your answer above cover all your relatives in the U. S. Government service? _____ (c) Which of the persons named above are temporarily employed? _____

16—10783

Guthrie's BPA job application

As the rating on education, training, or experience is largely determined from the information furnished in response to the questions asked in this form, each question should be FULLY and SPECIFICALLY yet concisely answered. When considering the qualifications of applicants, the Department must rigidly adhere to the prescribed specifications of education, training, or experience.

17. Give in the blanks below a detailed statement of your education, including dates:

(a) Grammar school: Attended from __Sept.__, 1918, to __June__, 1926   Highest grade completed __8th__

(b) High school: Name and location __Okemah High School, Okemah, Oklahoma__

Attended from __Sept.__, 926, to __June__, 929   Highest grade completed __10th__

Were you graduated? __No__

(c) College or university:

NAME	LOCATION	Dates of attendance (Give month and year) From—	To—	Semester hours credit received	Major subject Name	Sem. hrs. in majors	Degree conferred	Date of degree
None								

(d) If you have pursued any postgraduate courses of study, state fully what studies and when, where, and for what length of time they were pursued _____

(e) Name scholastic honors received __—__

(f) Name any publications of which you may be the author __—__

(g) If you are an applicant for an attorney or other legal position, answer the following questions: __—__

(1) Are you a bar member? __No__   (2) When and where were you admitted? _____

18. Furnish in blanks below a complete, comprehensive statement, showing every employment you have had since you first began to work, including your present employment, and accounting for all periods of unemployment. If you were in the military or naval service during the last five years and were stationed at any one point for six months or longer, give locations and dates to correspond for each period.

Places and dates of employment (Give city and State and month and year)	NAME AND ADDRESS OF EMPLOYER AND DEPARTMENT IN WHICH EMPLOYED (Give street address and city and State. If unemployed, give own address at that time)	NATURE OF YOUR DUTIES	Monthly salary	REASON FOR LEAVING (If discharged with prejudice explain on page 4.)
City and State Okemah, Okla. 1 From 9, 1928 To 6, 1929	George Meadors, Meadors Hotel	Night clerk & porter	$30	Called to Texas by illness in family.
City and State Pampa, Texas 2 From 7, 1929 To 7, 1929	Marvin Johnson, Root Beer Stand	Clerk	$90	Employer moved his business.
City and State Pampa, Texas 3 From 1929 To 1932	C. T. Harris, Harris Drug	Clerk and sign painter. Drove delivery truck.	$45	Discharged because of decrease in business.
City and State Pampa, Texas 4 From 1932 To 1934	Chas. Boozikee, Home Supply Market	Clerk, stocker, sign painter, & drove delivery truck.	$30	Terminated relations with business.
City and State Pampa, Texas 5 From 1934 To 1937	Unemployed 408 S. Russell St.	Played in a cowboy band.		
City and State Los Ang., Cal. 6 From 4, 1937 To 6, 1938	Frank Burke, Radio Station KFVD, Los Angeles, Calif.	30-minute program— collecting & presenting American folk songs	$30	Left to tour northern California.
City and State Calif. 7 From 6, 1938 To 12, 1938	Unemployed	Collected folk songs and stories.		
City and State Los Ang., Cal. 8 From 1, 1939 To 11, 1939	Frank Burke, Radio Station KFVD, Los Angeles, Calif.	30-minute program—collecting & presenting American folk songs.	$30	To New York to work for Tobacco Road Co.

IF MORE SPACE IS REQUIRED, PASTE SHEET OF PAPER ON THIS MARGIN, EXTEND COLUMN LINES, AND CONTINUE YOUR ENTRIES.

16—10782

but something that could touch the lives of people of four or five states and set a pattern for how democracy could function in this country with the government doing something constructive to improve the conditions of people."

Signed on to the project, Guthrie asked for one more thing: fifty cents to buy a hamburger. Kahn obliged.

Guthrie thrived in the framework laid out for him. He had an assignment, a purpose, doing what he did best—writing topical songs about things he cared about. He considered it a patriotic effort to promote something he deeply believed in: the government by the people, working for the people.

Guthrie instantly fell in love with both the Columbia River Gorge and the New Deal vision he was writing about. The sheer ruggedness of the region made it a far cry from the flat, dry plains of his upbringing. In a letter dated June 10, twenty-seven days into his assignment, he wrote friends in New York: "This Pacific Northwest is a country of wild rivers and rocky canyons and is one of the prettiest places you ever looked at. Uncle Sam is putting big power dams all along the rivers to produce electricity for public ownership and distribution through the people's utility districts in every town and countryside and the main job is to force the private-owned concerns to sell out to the government by selling power at lower rates."

Arlo Guthrie said the project was life-changing for his father. "He saw himself for the first time as being on the inside of a worthwhile, monumental, world-changing, nature-challenging, huge-beyond-belief thing. It was bigger than him, and frankly there weren't many things he considered bigger than him. Most people are the center of their own universe, and it's rare you get a chance to participate in something that you know is bigger than you and your country. He saw this as a big deal.

"He felt there was a real purpose here, an urgency," Arlo Guthrie said. "He believed what was happening here was not only good, but needed."

Beautiful country, an idealistic vision, and a demanding boss—it worked out to a perfect combination for Woody Guthrie. That month proved to be the most productive of his life: he wrote twenty-six songs in thirty days.

The monthlong job didn't make the Guthrie family flush, but it allowed them to rent a place with electricity and buy groceries—both improvements over their situation for the first part of the year so far. To get at the money in advance, Guthrie borrowed half of his coming wage from a federal employee loan office, which he said "only charged me $2.00 for a loan of $112.10."

"The ten bucks a day has enabled my wife and kids to exist on a status similar to humans and has produced for me the wherewithal to break quite a good number of the usual run of good health, good housekeeping and good behavior rules of accepted book learnt society," he wrote to friends that June.

He was apparently so taken with having his money that he made an odd show of it. One BPA employee recalled seeing him take a pencil rubbing of a silver dollar, then writing beneath it: "This dollar once belonged to Woody Guthrie."

The family spent a week in a cheap Portland auto camp before renting the northwest corner apartment on the bottom floor of a house at 6111 SE Ninety-Second Street for the rest of their stay. The house was in the working-class Lents neighborhood of Portland, and a full six miles from downtown Portland. Mary made fast friends with some neighbors, probably relieved to be around regular folks rather than the artistic class that made up the Guthries' social circle in Los Angeles and New York.

While Woody bragged to his friends that he was raising some hell with his newfound income, Mary Guthrie—who had every reason to cast Woody in the worst light possible—said he was particularly well behaved during his time in Portland, so consumed he was by his work.

"He wrote at night," Mary Guthrie said. "When Woody would come home, he always had notebooks and songs with him. He would go over these songs many times and I'm sure add more to them before the day was over." She added, "I was happy to be with him and enjoy a rather normal standard of living for a while."

But the job didn't solve all of Woody's money troubles.

One day, that blue Pontiac—bought on credit back when Woody Guthrie was a host on national radio not six months prior—turned up missing. When Guthrie told Kahn, Kahn asked him if he'd made payments on it.

"Well, I put a down payment," Guthrie responded.

"I can tell ya where that car is," Kahn said.

Kahn convinced Woody to shave off his beard to look more presentable to the finance company that had repossessed the beat-up sedan. However, when they spoke to the officer, he demanded $1,000, and with all the damage to the car, it was worth only half that much.

"You got that [much money], Woody?" Kahn asked. Upon hearing the answer, he tried to comfort the folksinger: "You didn't really want that car anyways, do ya?"

Guthrie said he didn't.

———————————

Despite Woody's colorful character traits, he gave Kahn little reason to regret his decision to put this "scruffy songwriter" on the government payroll.

From the outset, Guthrie showed an uncanny ability to absorb the complex history of and plans for the Columbia Basin and to distill it all into simple, catchy stanzas of verse.

"I gave him a book on the Columbia River and he produced two songs like you'd snap your fingers," Kahn recalled. Among those was the song "Roll On, Columbia," which he started writing his first day on the job, using the melody from Lead Belly's "Good Night Irene."

Buehler with state motor pool truck, 1972

"'Sheridan's boys in the blockhouse that night,' was a line telling
[...] troubles at Cascade Rapids and Phil Sheridan coming with
[...] Vancouver Barracks," Kahn said of the third stanza of that
[...]ng.

[...] later cut out the stanzas that glorified American military
[...] the indigenous peoples of the Northwest, but the point
[...] in twenty-four hours of arriving in town and being handed
[...] about the history of the area, he was putting the informa-
[...] into rhyming lyrics that have endured for seventy-five years.

Of course, Guthrie didn't simply sit in Portland, read books, and
write songs based on what the BPA told him. He struck out into the
country to see what all the fuss was about.

He wasn't trusted with a government car, Kahn said, considering
the sorry state of his Pontiac upon his arrival. Instead he was assigned
a driver—a man named Elmer Buehler.

932—MT. HOOD FROM LOST LAKE, OREGON

1A503-N

Postcard of Lost Lake, Oregon

Buehler, thirty, worked for Kahn in the public information office. One of his jobs was to drive around Washington and Oregon screening *Hydro*—the documentary Kahn had made for the BPA in 1939—at Grange halls, county fairs, and other public meetings. The job taught Buehler a strong sense of local geography. "It got to be that I knew every post office town in the Columbia Basin," he later said.

For the rest of his life, Buehler remembered those days on the road with Woody Guthrie. They were in a "shiny 1940 black Hudson Hornet," with Buehler at the wheel and Guthrie working on songs in the backseat.

"We didn't talk much, because he was always strumming his guitar and jotting notes," Buehler said. "He had a job to do."

Interestingly, one of the songs Buehler insisted he heard Guthrie play in the backseat was the ballad "This Land Is Your Land." Guthrie had written much of that song the year before, in 1940, while in New York, but he didn't put it into finished form until 1944, when he made his famous recording of it. Though it is not officially counted as one of the Columbia River ballads, Buehler's account suggests that the open roads of the Pacific Northwest prompted Guthrie to revisit the song extolling land for the people.

The Northwest was a wild country, like nothing Woody had ever seen, and the beauty had him awestruck. Buehler drove him east along the river and through the orchards of the Willamette Valley, then to visit the already-fading timber towns of Dee and Parkdale. But it was a side trip to Lost Lake, in the shadow of Mount Hood, that had perhaps the biggest impact. Surrounded on all sides by thick virgin forests, the lake was a revelation for Guthrie. "He just stood there in awe," Buehler recalled, "and he said, 'I've never seen anything like this. I am in paradise.'"

Woody worked what he saw into his new songs—cherries, peaches, apples, wheat, and other crops. He also saw hops for the first time, which must have thrilled him, considering how often he consumed its by-product.

As they drove along, they kept the windows down—Buehler said Guthrie had body odor, noting several times in his various interviews that his stench was often overpowering. As they traveled along the Columbia River Gorge and into the wide desert plains of Eastern Washington, Guthrie picked away at his songs. "He would play his guitar, apparently composing things as we drove along," Buehler said.

No definitive itinerary of Guthrie and Buehler's road trip exists, but they most likely followed the Columbia River into South-Central Washington, then crossed what was still an unirrigated expanse of desert to Spokane. From Spokane, it was a straight shot west to the Grand Coulee Dam site, where they could pick the river back up and follow it, more or less, all the way to Portland. With Buehler as guide, Guthrie saw the bucolic Willamette Valley; picturesque Hood River, in the gorge; Lake Chelan (Guthrie thought the Chelan River would be a great place for another dam); the apple orchards of Wenatchee; and, of course,

Ramblin' Blues (Portland Town)

Grand Coulee. Prior to the advent of the Interstate Highway System, it could be slowgoing on two-lane roads through the parched dun-colored country around the Columbia River, and they made many stops. Buehler took Woody to see factories and logging yards along the way. As planned, they also dropped in at Grange meetings and other gatherings, allowing Woody to meet the people and experience what they did.

"Rural people appealed to him," Buehler said. "Typically at a meeting, someone would come up and speak with Woody. Woody would listen and encourage the person."

In the tiny farm community of Arlington, Oregon, the two stopped for dinner at the local café. Presumably, Woody had his customary bowl of chili and leaned his guitar up against the counter. The sight of strangers in town—especially one with a guitar—was a curiosity, and soon Woody was singing to a small crowd. According to Buehler, this turned into an impromptu performance across the street at the local Grange hall. Soon word of mouth had the whole town coming down for a free night of entertainment.

Guthrie didn't extend such courtesies to everyone he met, however. In Spokane, he was asked to play "background music" for the local chamber of commerce. "I wouldn't play background music for any chamber of commerce, let alone foreground music," he sniffed.

Woody never wavered in his contempt for money traders, but this new "planned promised land" appealed to him. The tangible benefits of jobs, farming opportunities, and better living conditions were inspiring to him, and sparked a creative impulse.

Buehler's tour was effective in educating Guthrie not only about the landscape and the people, but also about the projects. He would later write, "I saw the Columbia River and the big Grand Coulee Dam from just about every cliff, mountain, tree and post from which it can be seen."

As he rode around the basin, the songs poured forth. "Some most fertile and pregnant ideas have occurred to me here," he wrote to friends.

It was just a year before that he'd recorded his *Dust Bowl Ballads* album, and the imagery of drought stricken Oklahoma was never far from Woody's mind. The Dust Bowl or the plight of migrant workers plays a role in at least twelve of the twenty-six Columbia River songs.

By Woody's telling, the Columbia Basin was the Eden folks had been "wastin' gasoline a'chasin' around." As he put it in "Washington Talkin' Blues":

> *Now what we need is a great big dam*
> *To throw a lot of water out acrost that land,*
> *People could work and the stuff would grow*
> *And you could wave goodbye to the old Skid Row.*

1940 black Hudson, similar to the one Guthrie and Buehler drove in the Columbia Basin

As it happened, on one of their trips they came upon a "vanguard of autos," as Buehler called it, carrying Dust Bowl refugees. There were "license plates from as far away as North and South Dakota driving toward the Willamette Valley, looking to get a better home. It was like seeing poverty on wheels." Guthrie was moved by the sight, telling his driver that those were "his people."

While Woody wisely followed Kahn's request in avoiding overtly political messages in his songs, perhaps the greatest song from his time on the Columbia River captures the bitterness held by the migrant farmers who had been destitute for nearly a decade: "Pastures of Plenty." From the outset of the song, he casts the American continent not as a land of promise, but as a harsh and indifferent world.

> *Out of your Dust Bowl and Westward we rolled*
> *And your deserts are hot and your mountains were cold*

It's from this perspective that the hope of transforming a dry basin into productive farmland truly comes through in Guthrie's work.

The version of the song recorded for the BPA film is a minor-key adaptation of the traditional standard "Pretty Polly," which, Alan Lomax wrote, has a "starkly brooding melody" that "endows 'Pastures of Plenty' with somber melancholy."

> *Look down in the canyon and there you will see*
> *The Grand Coulee showers her blessings on me;*
> *The lights for the city, for factory, and mill*
> *Green pastures of plenty from dry barren hills.*

Arguably, no government report, study, or memo ever captured the intent of the Columbia Basin Project better than "Pastures of Plenty."

In a similar vein, Guthrie found hope in the Grand Coulee Dam.

Mary Guthrie said that Woody was "fascinated by the dam," an assertion clearly backed up by his songs. Guthrie broke into hyperbole when singing about the enormous structure, in one song calling it "the biggest thing that man has ever done" and in another, "the mightiest thing ever built by man."

The dam was a perfect backdrop for Guthrie to tell the story of the common workers: the "powder monkeys," the jackhammer men, the drillers. "We come a long ways, it was looking for work, all along down the wide highway you see, and this loafing 'round idle is really what hurts," he writes in "Guys on the Grand Coulee Dam."

Grand Coulee powder monkeys and jackhammer johns at work, 1930s

As the nation emerged from the worst depression in its history, Guthrie saw the Grand Coulee as irrefutable proof of the value and might of the American worker. That this work was going toward providing electricity to factories producing war materials that would soon be taking on Nazi forces lent a patriotic flavor to many of the songs, such as "Biggest Thing That Man Has Ever Done":

There's a man across the ocean, boys, I guess you know him well
His name is Adolf Hitler, we'll blow his soul to hell;
We'll kick him in the panzers and put him on the run,
And that'll be the biggest thing that man has ever done.

Little about the federal programs along the river went unmentioned by Guthrie in his twenty-six songs. He addresses rural electrification in "End of My Line" ("But there ain't no country extra fine, / If you're just a mile from the end o' the line"); trade being facilitated by the locks at the Bonneville Dam in "Talking Columbia" ("Gasoline a goin' up. Wheat a-comin' down"); and, of course, electricity itself in "Eleckatricity and All."

In his ballads, little distinction is drawn between hydropower and the river itself. Rather, the electricity "Uncle Sam" was harnessing from the Columbia was a pure manifestation of nature being used to improve citizens' lives.

There's undoubtedly a something-for-nothing quality to Guthrie's Columbia River work, a suggestion that damming the Columbia wouldn't diminish the wild character of the river he was clearly in love with. "Now river, you can ramble where the sun sets in the sea / But while you're rambling, river, you can do some work for me," Guthrie sings in "Roll, Columbia, Roll." At the same time, one has to marvel at the way Guthrie's driving ballads so clearly convey the simple truth of the matter: that one of the great forces of nature on the North American continent was now channeling the miracle of electricity across a huge swath of the Pacific Northwest. The driving waltz of "Roll On, Columbia" clearly invokes the cascading waters of the river itself: "Your power is turning our darkness to dawn, / Roll on, Columbia, roll on!"

Of course, some lyrics don't stand up to modern scrutiny, specifically, the celebration of the Native American wars in "Roll On, Columbia" that today are recognized as a near-genocidal government policy. In addressing the controversial lyrics, Arlo Guthrie said

his father later "scratched them out and didn't use them." Buehler's account of Woody's time in the Northwest suggests he didn't hold any ill will toward Native Americans. Rather, one of his favorite parts of the trip was meeting tribal members at Celilo Falls, which was an even larger salmon-fishing area than Kettle Falls was. At the falls, fishermen would perch precariously over the raging waters on what looked like rickety wooden docks in order to snag salmon with dip nets. Celilo Falls was eventually drowned by the completion of The Dalles Dam in 1957, but at the time it was still an important gathering spot.

Celilo Falls before The Dalles Dam submerged the ancient fishing and trading post in 1957

"He was very much interested in the Indians that were up there. He looked upon them as the common people too," said Buehler.

Guthrie also expressed sympathy for Native Americans in personal correspondence. If he was ignorant of the effects government development on the river was having on salmon, he was keen to its industrial harms. "Some factories are dumping refuse & chemical garbage into the nation's greatest salmon, power stream, the Columbia River," he wrote. "Millions of fish are destroyed and the Indians are plenty sore. The dried salmon mean grub for the hard winter. . . . All running water is public property under federal law—why this poisoning of the river?"

When he wasn't on the road, Guthrie was given a desk in the corner of the BPA's public information office. He was generally well liked in the office. According to witnesses, he was "free and easy in his conversation with everybody and was completely uninhibited—but he was diamond sharp."

Still, the unusual nature of Guthrie's work led to unusual scenes there. He banged out rhythms on his metal desk, quite a distraction to other employees, and his body odor remained an issue; Buehler claimed several of the BPA secretaries complained about the stench that emanated from the new employee. Guthrie didn't hesitate to strike up conversations around the office. And he'd sometimes sit on the corner of Kahn's desk and hash out folk tunes, Kahn humming along as Guthrie strummed his guitar.

Pete Seeger called his way of writing music the "scatteration technique."

"His method of composition was to pound out verse after verse on the typewriter or in his precise country-style handwriting, and try it out on his guitar as he went along," Seeger said.

That was definitely the case with the Columbia River ballads.

Like he always did, Guthrie used existing melodies to write his new topical songs—about the Columbia, the New Deal, the Oregon Trail, "eleckatricity," and migrants trying to get a little piece of land of their own. Not to mention "them salmon fish," which are "mighty shrewd." "Just like a president, they run ever' four years," he says in "Talking Columbia."

Kahn didn't mind that the melodies weren't new, nor did he mind if Woody turned in a new version of a song he had written previously. There were many of them– including "Hard Travelin'," "It Takes a Married Man," and "Jackhammer Blues"—in which Woody altered the lyrics and wrote in some local color. It was the folk process, which came in handy

"He could write a song about a subject and do it in the styles of the old songs, so people could play along almost instantly. This was the great feature about this stuff," said Arlo Guthrie. "And that's what my dad did with these Columbia River songs. He took these old tunes and styles and put new words in them, and they were sort of instantly fit in your ear."

When a song was finished, Woody went into the closet in the BPA's basement and recorded low-quality demos.

Kahn wasn't impressed with all the work, saying that "some of them were pretty poor."

Still, in sum he was happy with the product—if a bit unappreciative of how far the music would travel outside Portland

"I thought Woody's songs would be very effective in reaching the common man," Kahn said. "I didn't envision that they would become nationally popular, because I was not aware fully of what the people were listening to or what they were singing, but I recognized talent there, originality and personality."

Guthrie, too, seemed happy with his work. On June 10, he wrote to friends that while the job wasn't going to last as long as he wanted, it was still very productive. He seemed particularly excited to have started writing about electricity, along with his more standard Dust Bowl fare.

"My visit to Oregon and Washington has not been of no avail but on the contrary has furnished me with not only an array of scenic material

Ramblin' Blues (Portland Town)

equal to an ordinary book but has also supplied me with five or six new ballads of an electrical, I mean industrial character," he wrote.

Notably, in the same letter he wrote that he'd filled out his military draft papers—another premonition of war to come.

In another letter, he wrote to his future collaborators in the Almanac Singers about how adding details of labor would authenticate such "work songs."

"You ought to throw in more wheels, triggers, springs, bearings, motors, engines, boilers, and factories," he said, "because these are the things that arm the workers and these are the source of the final victory of Public Ownership."

Guthrie was seemingly sold not only on the project and the future of public utilities, but on the idea that working men and women were going to get the country out of Depression living, fight fascism, and win the ensuing war.

On May 28, 1941, paperwork was filed to establish Guthrie's last time of employment with the BPA as noon on June 13. The files show he'd accrued "2 days, 3 hours and 30 minutes" of leave time and specify that he would begin taking his leave at eight thirty a.m. on June 11.

On June 10, Guthrie wrote friends in New York that he'd be heading their way soon. With his car still in the impound lot, his plan was to hitchhike.

Caring for their three kids, ages eighteen months to five years, Mary was staying put in Portland. She kept their 6111 SE Ninety-Second Street place for the rest of the summer, which she looked back upon as thoroughly enjoyable.

"We had a pretty good time," she'd later recall. When it got close to the beginning of the school year, she and the kids headed to Los Angeles, and from there to El Paso. While there, she pawned Woody's typewriter for five dollars.

"I had to have money for my kids," she said, explaining her reasoning.

She and Woody never lived under the same roof again, and by the fall they were officially separated. They divorced in March of 1943.

On June 11, Guthrie started walking down the highway that followed the course of the river that he now knew so well, a guitar over his back and a thumb in the air. Just outside Portland, a young lawyer named Gus Solomon pulled up alongside the folksinger. He was the BPA's lawyer at the time and had met Guthrie at the offices. "Woody, where are you going?" Solomon asked.

"I'm going to New York," he said.

"How will you get there?"

"I'm going to hitchhike," Guthrie said without any note of irony.

"Do you have any money?" Solomon asked.

Guthrie said he did not.

Broke as the day he got there, Guthrie accepted twenty dollars and a ride to The Dalles. From there, he continued on east, where there were more songs to be sung.

So long, it's been good to know yuh.

Roll Columbia

There's a great and peaceful river in a land that is fair to see
Where the Douglas fir tree whispers to the snow capped mountain breeze.
The cliffs are solid granite and the valley's always green,
This is just as close to heavy as my traveling feet have been.

> Roll Columbia, won't you roll, roll, roll
> Roll Columbia, won't you roll, roll, roll.

Stand upon her timbered mountain, look across her silver strand,
See the crops and orchards springing to the touch of nature's hand.
And it's farther up the river where your eye will meet the skies
Where you'll see the steel and concrete of the Grand Coulee rise.

Chorus

There at Priest and Cascade rapids men have labored day and night,
Matched their strength against the river in its wild and reckless flight.
Boats and rafts were beat to splinters but it left men dreams to dream
Of that day when they would conquer the wild and wasted stream.

Chorus

Uncle Sam took up the challenge in the year of '33
For the farmers and the workers and for all humanity.
Now river you can ramble where the sun sets in the sea,
But while you're rambling river you can do some work for me.

Chorus

Now there's full a million horses charged with Coulee's 'lectric power
Day and night they'll run the factory and they never will get tired.
Well a coal mine gets dug out and an oil well it runs dry,
But Uncle Sam will find his power where the river meets the sky.

Chorus

CHAPTER 7

ROLL, COLUMBIA, ROLL

A s Woody pressed onnt to New York City to join the Almanac Singers for a national tour,* there were doubts that the documentary he was hired on to help with would ever get made.

Even before he left for New York, Guthrie griped in a letter, "Our script . . . must be okayed in Wash., D.C. before we can get a go ahead sign on the regular film, which I hold very doubtful because of many reasons."

In reality, the full feature film made strong headway over the next few months after Guthrie's time in Portland. The Bureau of Reclamation—which managed the Grand Coulee Dam—agreed to help the BPA with the cost of the film "after six weeks of arguing back in Washington," according to Kahn. It wasn't really enough money, he said, but they went ahead and filmed scenes for the documentary anyway.

About six months after Woody left Portland, in early 1942, Kahn traveled to New York City to arrange for some of the Columbia River ballads to be recorded professionally for use in the film. Recorded were "Roll, Columbia, Roll"; the minor-key version of "Pastures of Plenty," which differed significantly from the well-known major-key version that entered the Woody Guthrie canon; and "Biggest Thing That Man Has Ever Done." Kahn said the government gave him twenty dollars to

* Ironically, the 1941 Almanac tour headed west from New York, and while the group headed home after dates in California, Pete Seeger and Guthrie continued to Portland and Seattle in September. The image of Guthrie (see page vi) overlooking the Pacific Ocean is presumably from this trip, taken somewhere in Oregon.

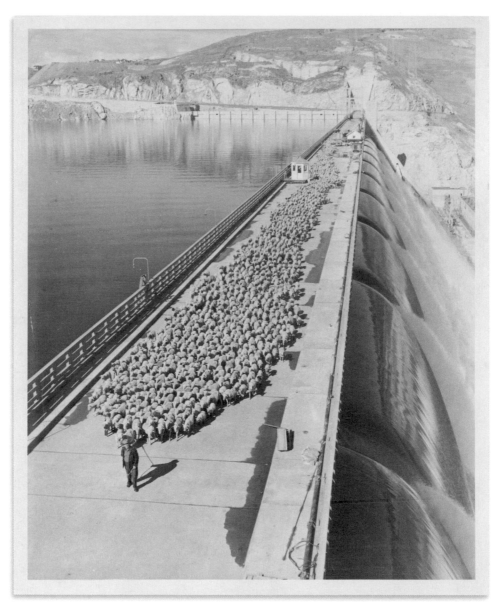

*Old world meets new world as wool grower Joe Hodgkin and
2,600 sheep cross the Grand Coulee Dam, 1947*

pay Woody for the recording session—held at Reeves Sound Studios—but that the folksinger impressed him so much he gave him a ten-dollar tip and treated him to a meal at a French restaurant as a thank-you.

"I took him to a fancy . . . really, a reasonably fancy restaurant on Fifty-Second Street, and Woody looked over the menu, which was mostly in French, and he says, 'Bring me a 'amburger,'" Kahn recalled. "The French waiter says, 'We do not have ze ham-bare-gare.' . . . And he says, 'Steve, ya know, I'll take you down to the Village, and for fifteen cents you can get an Oklahoma hamburger that's better than all this crap they're serving here.' That was typical of Woody."

But with the bombing of Pearl Harbor on December 7, 1941, the United States had joined the war. At the BPA, as with all other government agencies, energies were soon being directed entirely to the war effort. The public information office churned out a quick documentary about the Liberty ships being produced in Portland with Bonneville electricity. "Power from the Columbia River is building the ships and planes to defend the land we love," was the new refrain of the agency. Kahn shelved the footage that had been shot and the soundtrack he'd recorded with Guthrie, with hopes of putting the feature film together when the war ended.

Kahn eventually went to Europe with the army and crossed the English Channel to fight, noting later that he had marveled at how America's air force—built largely with aluminum manufactured in the Northwest with cheap hydropower—had all but vanquished the Nazi Luftwaffe. He also, coincidentally, rode in an army boat named after the late J. D. Ross.

Meanwhile, Gunther von Fritsch joined the signal corps and was tapped to make a government film about Franklin D. Roosevelt's dog. *Fala: The President's Dog* came out in 1943.

Woody himself served with the merchant marines three times between 1942 and 1945; the army eventually drafted him in 1945, one month before Germany surrendered.

When the war was over, Kahn's hopes for getting right back to his feature film proved to be overly optimistic.

World War II left the United States a completely different nation than the one he and Woody Guthrie had written about in 1941. Kahn had hoped that *The Columbia* would be "like *The Grapes of Wrath*, which changed attitudes in this country." With victory secured, the plight of Dust Bowl farmers was a subject a newly optimistic nation cared not to dwell on. Kahn returned to his job at the BPA but didn't return to the material gathered for his documentary for four years.

It wasn't until 1948, when a massive flood of the Columbia inundated the Oregon city of Vanport, also known as Kaiserville, that Kahn saw an opportunity to resurrect the film. Vanport was essentially a public housing project developed in a floodplain to give shelter to the thousands of workers who had flocked to Portland to work in Henry Kaiser's shipyards. Nearly fifty thousand people lived in the 648-acre development, with a disproportionately large black population owing to the fact that many neighborhoods in Portland didn't allow African American residents. On Memorial Day in 1948, a surging river breached a dike that kept the waters out of Vanport and flooded the homes of eighteen thousand people, 40 percent of whom were African American. Fifteen people were killed by the flood, and the entire city was considered a loss.

The devastation was bad enough that President Harry Truman toured the area. The news also caught Guthrie's attention. In a letter to a friend in Portland in July 1948, Guthrie complained about his housing situation—a recurring theme in his life—then suggested he had nothing to gripe about. "Can we even worry about a wall around us," he wrote, "so long as we stand in our thoughts there within eyeshot of the wartown of Vanport where so many thousands of families got their houses knocked down into kindling wood by the same old Columbia River I was singing so many good things about. I think the lack of flood control and power dams that caused this flood to break will give us all plenty to make up songs and to sing about for the rest of our native lives."

Aerial view of the aftermath of the Vanport Flood, May 30, 1948

Kahn's thinking was very similar to Woody's. In the late 1940s, many of the same debates over public power were still consuming the Pacific Northwest, among them whether the federal government should build more dams on the Columbia. Kahn saw the Vanport flood as helping the case for dams: more dams meant more flood control, so in his mind the more dams, the better. He said he decided to resurrect the film project "and give Woody another chance to see daylight with those songs."

The film finally came out in 1949 with little fanfare. It wasn't the ambitious feature film once envisioned, running just twenty-one minutes and reusing much of the footage shot for *Hydro*. Three songs—"Roll, Columbia, Roll," "Pastures of Plenty," and "Biggest Thing That Man Has Ever Done" are used in the film. But most of the soundtrack relies on reuse of the orchestral soundtrack to *Hydro*. While the Vanport flood

Roll, Columbia, Roll

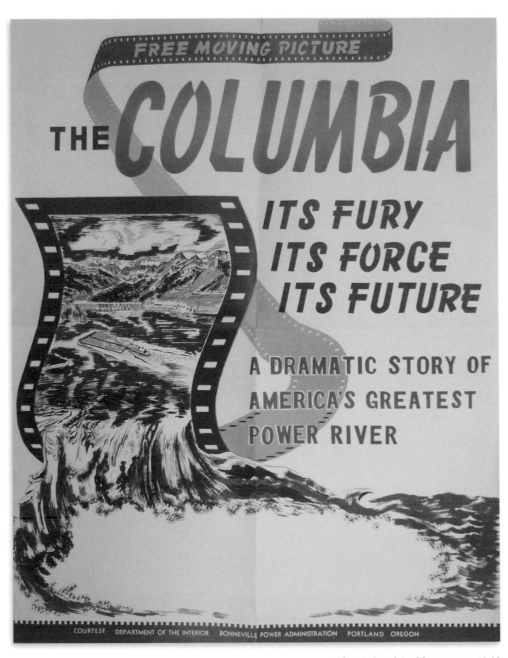

The Columbia *film poster, 1949*

had spurred Kahn back into action, he retained much of the narrative that he and Guthrie had established: the Columbia River projects offered a grand solution to problems that plagued America in the 1930s and beyond. Indeed, the film's soaring rhetoric seems to make the dubious suggestion that it was Dust Bowl refugees themselves who dreamed up the Grand Coulee Dam irrigation project in the first place.

"The migrants came to the heart of the Columbia River Basin to find land as burned and useless as the dust-stricken acres they had left behind. . . . An endless string of refugees from the Dust Bowl gazed at the arid acres and moved on. Broken wagon wheels, bleached cattle bones, were warning enough," the narrator booms as scenes of rolling tumbleweeds and abandoned buildings in the Washington desert are shown. "If they were to find land, they must first bring the Columbia water to the lifeless acres. And Grand Coulee Dam was the answer."

The movie does lend some striking visual context to Guthrie's music. In particular, Kahn paired footage of a Dust Bowl family leaving its ruined farm with Guthrie singing the sad opening of "Pastures of Plenty." And "Biggest Thing That Man Has Ever Done" is played over footage of the construction of the Grand Coulee Dam, celebrating the feat of engineering and construction.

Modern viewers may find it rewarding to hear Woody Guthrie's songs in this context. At the time of its release, though, it made very little impact on the public and was hardly a vehicle for popularizing Guthrie's Columbia River ballads.

Rather, as he often did, Guthrie revisited the songs and found other uses for them.

For example, on Christmas Day 1944, NBC broadcast "America for Christmas" on its *Cavalcade of America* radio show. The episode followed a fictional singing troupe that performed for homesick GIs on a remote South Pacific island. Among the songs performed are "Hard Travelin'," "Grand Coulee Dam," and "Pastures of Plenty," and the chorus of "Roll On, Columbia." Guthrie himself didn't sing on the program—

Moe Asch of Smithsonian Folkways, New York City

Earl Robinson sang lead on most of the songs, but Woody's songs were getting heard.

Also in 1944, Guthrie initiated a relationship with independent record-maker Moe Asch, who eventually released Guthrie's Columbia River songs commercially. Asch, who started a variety of different labels over the years (including Disc, Stinson, and Folkways), developed a close relationship with Guthrie and granted him a nearly open-door policy at his New York recording studios. Woody either came in alone with a harmonica, or with collaborators like Cisco Houston and Sonny Terry. Because of poorly kept records, there is limited information about these recording sessions. Over the years, there have been attempts to create an accepted discography, but for the most part Woody's scatteration effect was in play during his relationship with Asch. Still, it's known that between 1944 and 1947, Guthrie conducted more than a dozen sessions in which he recorded or rerecorded a number of Columbia River songs.

By early 1947, despite their not having been released commercially, the songs seemed to have gained some traction in the Pacific Northwest. In spring of that year, Guthrie traveled to Spokane at the invitation of the BPA's Ralph Bennett as a guest at a convention of the National Rural Electric Cooperative Association. The appearance in Spokane didn't go well, but while there he was pleased to hear that his songs were making the rounds. From Spokane, he wrote to Asch in hopes of persuading him to produce an album of Columbia River songs. "They want to see you

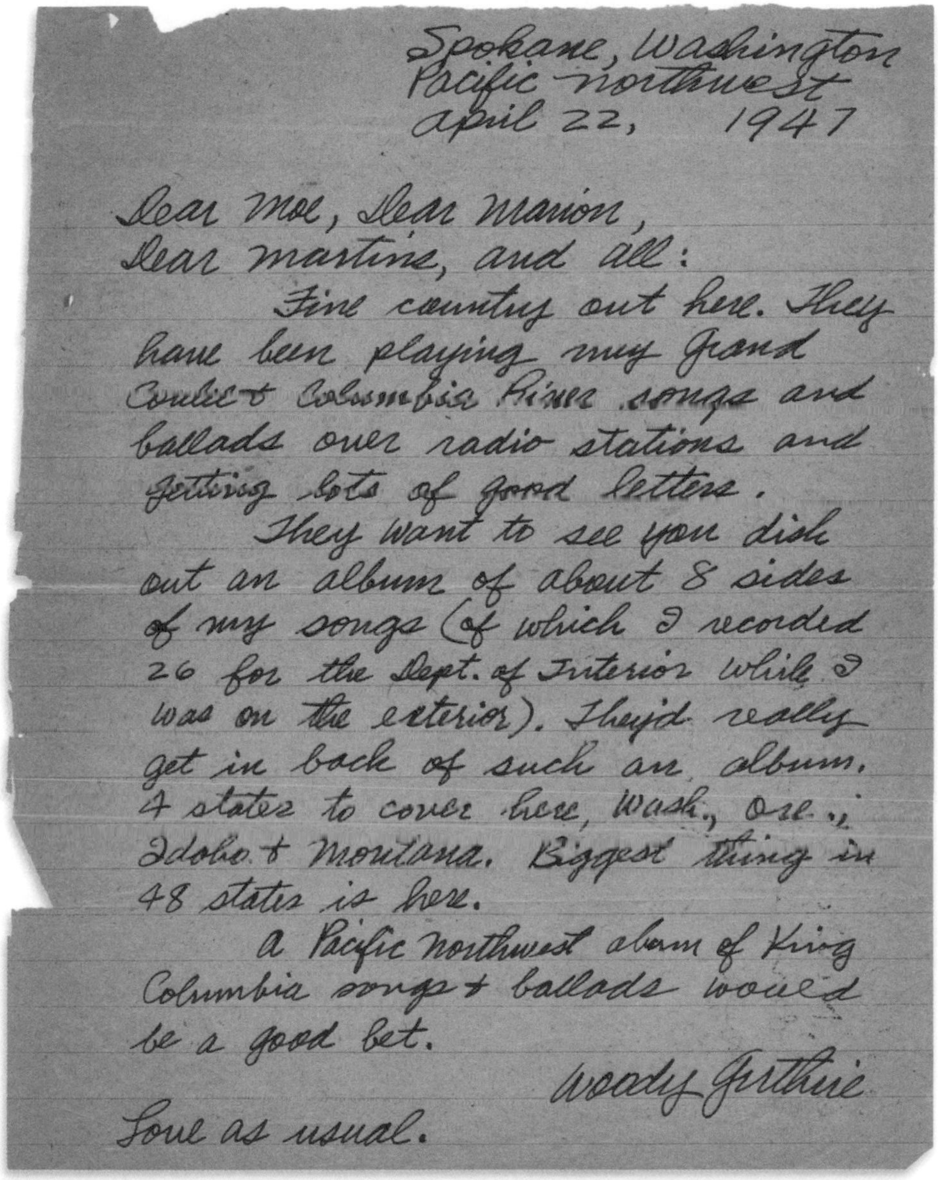

Spokane, Washington
Pacific northwest
April 22, 1947

Dear Moe, Dear Marion,
Dear martins, and all:

Fine country out here. They
have been playing my Grand
Coulee & Columbia River songs and
ballads over radio stations and
getting lots of good letters.

They want to see you dish
out an album of about 8 sides
of my songs (of which I recorded
26 for the Dept. of Interior while I
was on the exterior). They'd really
get in back of such an album.
4 states to cover here, Wash., Ore.,
Idaho & Montana. Biggest thing in
48 states is here.

A Pacific northwest album of King
Columbia songs & ballads would
be a good bet.

Woody Guthrie

Love as usual.

Woody's letter to Moe Asch from Spokane, Washington, 1947

dish out an album of about 8 sides of my songs (of which I recorded 26 for the Dept. of Interior while on the exterior)," Woody wrote.

Asch was persuaded. When Guthrie returned, they recorded "Pastures of Plenty," "End of My Line," "Hard Travelin'," "New Found Land," "Oregon Trail," "Ramblin' Round," "Talking Columbia," and "Columbia Talking Blues." Shortly after, Disc released the first album of Columbia River songs.

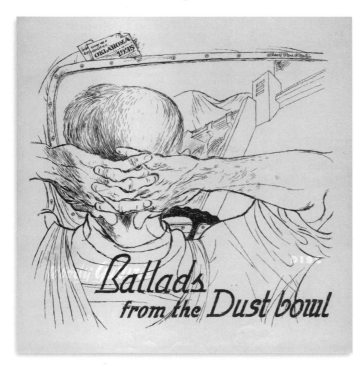

Ballads from the Dust Bowl *album cover, DISC Records, 1947*

This obscure and now out-of-print album was called *Ballads from the Dust Bowl*, perhaps an allusion to the heavy influence the Dust Bowl had on Guthrie's outlook on the Columbia River projects. It could also have been a simple marketing ploy to play off Guthrie's Great Depression brand. Either way, the album art is more to the point: an illustration of a man comfortably reclining in his car as he gazes at the giant Grand Coulee Dam.

Conspicuously absent from both the Asch recording sessions and the Disc album is "Roll On, Columbia," which Guthrie seems to have largely forgotten about by the late 1940s.

In 1948, Guthrie wrote to a folksinger and former BPA employee in Portland named Michael Loring, asking him for the lyrics to "Roll On, Columbia." Pete Seeger had asked Guthrie for the words for inclusion in one of his People's Songs songbooks. (People's Songs eventually morphed into *Sing Out!*, one of the most influential publications in American folk music throughout the mid-twentieth century.) At the time of his letter, Guthrie said he was working at a "daycamp for kids," which he said was "just about as far north as you can get without tromping your foot down on the fascist side of the Canadian boundary line." Guthrie asked Loring to send Seeger the lyrics to the song, as he himself had forgotten most of them and didn't have his songbook handy. In fact, the letter suggests that Guthrie had trouble even remembering which song "Roll On, Columbia" was "I think this is the ballad one, the one that goes: 'The Indians we killed there at Coe's little store,'" he wrote, choosing perhaps the most unfortunate stanza to cite. In a bit of irony, Guthrie also jokes about making sure Seeger doesn't add any of his own lyrics to the song; as it turned out, Loring added a new stanza to the song, which has become standard-use to this day.

> Tom Jefferson's vision would not let him rest
> An empire he saw in the Pacific Northwest.
> Sent Lewis and Clark and they did the rest;
> Roll on, Columbia, roll on.

Guthrie never commercially recorded the song, and yet it seemed destined early on to retain a vaunted spot in the pantheon of American folk music.

In the June 28, 1948, issue of the *New Republic*, none other than former vice president and third-party presidential candidate Henry Wallace cited the song in a column he penned about the importance of folk music in America.

"I am now becoming convinced that when the people are deeply moved by the impulse to take constructive action, they sing. When they are afraid, the spirit of song dies away," Wallace writes. Later he continues, "One impressive Western singer, for both his voice and his personality, is Mike Loring of Portland, Oregon. We loved hearing him sing:

"ROLL ON, COLUMBIA, ~~ROLL ON~~"
(a regional Folk Song)

Green Douglas fir where the waters cut through,
Down her wild mountains and canyons she flew,
Canadian Northwest to the ocean so blue,
It's roll on Columbia, Roll on!

    Roll on, Columbia, roll on!
    Roll on, Columbia, roll on!
    Your power is turning our darkness to dawn;
    Roll on, Columbia, roll on!

Other great rivers add power to you,
Yakima, Snake, and the Klickitat, too,
Sandy, Willamette and Hood River, too;
Roll on Columbia, roll on!

        Chorus

Tom Jefferson's vision would not let him rest--
An empire he saw in the Pacific Northwest!
Sent Lewis and Clark and they did the rest
So roll on, Columbia, roll on!

These mighty men labored by day and by night
Matching their strength 'gainst the river's wild flight,
Through rapids and falls they won the hard fight
Roll on, Columbia, roll on!

        Chorus

At Bonneville Dam there are ~~boats~~ ships covered in the locks,
The waters have risen and ~~cleared all~~ the rocks,
Ship loads of plenty will steam past your docks,
So roll on, Columbia, roll on!

        Chorus

And far up the river is Grand Coulee dam,
The mightiest thing ever built by a man,
To run the great factories and water the land,
It's roll on, Columbia, roll on!

        Chorus

Pete—have used these two verses (my own) For clubs, etc. where the detailed historical allusions in woody's middle Verses were tougher to get across.

Michael Loring's revision of Guthrie's "Roll On, Columbia"
sent to Pete Seeger's organization People's Songs upon
Guthrie's request in 1948

Roll on, Columbia, roll on.
Your power is turning our darkness to dawn.

"This song has a tune which even the tuneless can sing," Wallace writes. "It gives a wonderful sense of the restless might of a great river. I am told that the private-power interests of the Northwest do not like this song, because they feel that the second line may somehow be subversive of their best interest."

While Wallace credits Loring for singing him the song—no doubt that was true—the editors of the magazine state at the bottom of the page that the lyrics were used with permission of Woody Guthrie.

Thus, it seems, Loring had a vital role in popularizing this song, keeping it alive even as Guthrie forgot about it.

It is a testament to the power of the folk tradition that over the next decade-plus "Roll On, Columbia" spread far and wide in American society without the benefit of a commercial recording until 1960. At the fiftieth convention of the International Union of Mine, Mill and Smelter Workers, held in Spokane in 1955, one attendee suggested that union workers sing the song to Congress to persuade it to approve more dam projects. The notetaker at the convention reported that this suggestion was greeted with applause. In a play about the history of the Pacific Northwest published in 1960, the playwright punctuates the moment that Captain Robert Gray names the river Columbia by having his crew sing "Roll On, Columbia"—despite the implausibility of eighteenth-century sailors singing about electricity. In 1958, a writer in the folk music magazine *Caravan* states that while Guthrie wrote "several dozen" songs for the BPA, it was "'Roll On, Columbia' which seems destined to last for generations." That seemed all but assured, as the song began appearing in a number of children's songbooks starting in the 1950s. This explains why most people who know "Roll On, Columbia" learned it not by hearing it on the radio but in school and summer camp. In fact, when the song was finally released in 1960, it appeared on a record that

(THIS STONECREST LODGE IS A RADICAL WORKING CLASS ISLAND UP HERE IN A LAKE OF DEAD MONEYBELLIES).

JULY 9th, 1948

LORING FAMILY:
DEAR EVERYBODY:

PEOPLES SONGS WROTE TO ME AND ASKED FOR THE WORDS AND MUSIC TO THE SONG "ROLL ON COLUMBIA, ROLL ON". (I THINK THIS IS THE BALLAD ONE, THE ONE THAT GOES:

THE INDIANS WE KILLED THERE AT COE'S LITTLE STORE
BY FIREBALL AND RIFLE A DOZEN OR MORE
WE WERE SAVED BY THE MARY AND SOLDIERS SHE BORE
ROLL ON COLUMBIA, ROLL ON.   (CHORUS)

MARJORIE AND ARLO DAVY AND ME ARE UP HERE JUST ABOUT AS FAR NORTH AS YOU CAN GET WITHOUT TROMPING YOUR FOOT DOWN ON THE FASCIST SIDE OF THE CANADAIAN BOUNDARY LINE. WE'RE WORKING UP HERE AT A DAYCAMP FOR KIDS FOR THESE NEXT TWO MONTHS TILL THE FIRST WEEK IN SEPTEMBER. (OUR HOUSE AIN'T SO HOT, IT'S JUST A ONE ROOMER BEING BUILT UP AROUND OUR HEADS RIGHT NOW, BUT WITH NO HOT WATER IT'S QUITE A HEADACHE, OR CAN WE EVEN WORRY ABOUT A WALL AROUND US, SO LONG AS WE STAND IN OUR THOUGHTS THERE WITHIN EYESHOT OF THE WARTOWN OF VANPORT WHERE SO MANY THOUSANDS OF FAMILIES GOT THEIR HOUSES KNOCKED DOWN INTO KINDLING WOOD BY THE SAME OLD COLUMBIA RIVER I WAS SINGING SO MANY GOOD THINGS ABOUT. I THINK THE LACK OF FLOOD CONTROL AND POWER DAMS THAT CAUSED THIS FLOOD TO BREAK WILL GIVE US ALL PLENTY TO MAKE UP SONGS AND TO SING ABOUT FOR THE REST OF OUR NATIVE LIVES.

I'D SURE APPRECIATE IT IF YOU'D GRAB UP THE WORDS TO THIS SONG, ROLL ON COLUMBIA, AND SHOOT THEM BY HIGH AIR MAIL OVER TO THE PEOPLES SONGS OFFICE IN NEW YORK CITY. THEY WANT TO RUN THE SONG IN CONNECTION WITH A STORY OF SOME KIND ABOUT YOU AND THE REST OF THE SINGERS ALL OVER THE PACIFIC NORTHWEST. I JUST FAILED TO BRING THE SONGBOOK UP WITH ME WHICH HAS GOT MY GRAND COULEE SONGS IN IT, AND SO, AM JUST UP A SLICK ROOT TREE, CAN'T SEND THE WORDS NOR A DAM THING. PETE SEEGER SAYS THAT HE KNOWS THE MELODY LINES, BUT I'LL GET MARJORIE TO JOT THEM DOWN SO'S PETE CAN'T STRAY OFF ACROST THE MUDBANK NOWHERE. ALL YOU'VE GOT TO DO IS TO SEND PS A COPY OF THE WORDS AS QUICK AS YOU CAN, SINCE IT DOES TAKE A BIT OF TIME TO GET ALL OF THESE THINGS FOTO OFFSAT AND REDUCED AND ENLARGED AND SO FORTH FOR THE PS BULLETIN.

THIS IS SURE ONE PRETTY COUNTRY, BUT A STRIP WHICH IS FULL OF SOME OF THE RICHEST SILLIEST LOOKING EMPTY OLD HOTELS WHICH YOU EVER SEEN, A SUMMER SOLDIER COUNTRY, A FAREPAYING STRANGER GREEN SUMMER GRASS PLACE FOR A QUICK SQUAT AND A HARD RUN BACK TO THE SOUTHLAND WHENEVER THE FIRST THREATS OF COLD WEATHER HITS YOU ON YOUR NOSE. BUT THESE WHITE MOUNTAINS ARE PLENTY OLD AND PRETTY ENOUGH TO STAND RIGHT HERE THROUGH ALL OF OUR EARTHLY MISTAKES AND WAIT TILL WE CAN RIP THROUGH TEN MORE CENTURIES OF CHAINS OF ALL KINDS TO FIND SOME HONEST WORKING KIDS, MAS, PAS, AND WORKING FOLKS TO FILL UP ALL OF THESE SKI MOUNTAINS ALL THE YEAR ROUND.

THANKS A LOT FOR THE TROUBLE I'VE ASKED YOU TO SEND PS THIS COLUMBIA RIVER SONG. I HOPE THISFINDS YOU FINE AND DANDY AND FITTEN AS A KITTEN PLAYING WITH A LEATHER MITTEN.

LOVE
US GUTHRIES

ARLO DAVY
MARJORIE
WOODY

Woody

I can still hear you singing you found land

accompanied a school book. Not until 1963 did the song appear on an album meant for adults, when the Highwaymen (the folk group, not the country supergroup) and the Homesteaders both released a version of the song.

By this time, the song had already gained wide popularity. This is proven beyond a doubt by another early recording of the song, a rendition that the Weavers performed live at their reunion concert at Carnegie Hall in 1963.

As they sang it, it was actually a medley, opening with a verse from "Roll, Columbia, Roll" and segueing into the chorus for "Roll On, Columbia." Neither song had ever been a Billboard hit, and the concert was a long way from the Northwest. But the New York City audience obviously knew the second song.

As the fairly obscure "Roll, Columbia, Roll" was sung, the crowd remained quiet. But when once the waltz of "Roll On, Columbia" set in, it was greeted with enthusiastic applause.

I'M A GONNA HIT THAT OREGON LINE
THIS COMIN' FALL

I been a grubbin' on a little farm
On them flat and windy plains
And a listenin to them hungry cattle bawl;
I'm a gonna pack my wife and children
And We'll strike the western road
And we'll hit that Oregon trail this comin' fall.

  I'm a gonna hit that Oregon trail this comin' Fall,
  I'm a gonna hit that Oregon trail this comin' Fall,
  Where the good rain falls a plenty,
  Where the crops and orchards grow;
  I'm a gonna hit that Oregon trail this comin' fall.

Well, my land is dry and crackling
And my chickens they are cackling
'Cause the dirt and dust is a gettin' in their craw;
They been a layin' flint rock eggs,
You got to bust them with a sledge,
And I got to hit that Oregon trail this comin' Fall.

Yes, my hogs and pigs a squealin'
They're a rockin' and a reelin'
'Cause there aint no mud to waller in the draw;
I'm a gonna grab one by his tail
And take him down that western trail,
And we'll hit the Oregon trail this comin' fall.

Now my good old horse is bony,
Yes, he's dry and hungry, too,
You can see his ribs three quarters of a mile;
Throw 6 kids up on his back,
Both the bay horse and the black,
And we'll hit that Oregon trail this comin' Fall.

Oh, my wife gets sort of ailin'
When that mean old dust's a sailin',
And she wishes for the days beyond recall;
If we work hard there's a future
In that North Pacific land,
So we'll hit that Oregon Trail this comin' Fall.

Woody Guthrie
Bonneville Power Adm.,
US Dept Interior
811 N.E. Oregon St.,
Portland, Ore.
5-14-1941

CHAPTER 8

OREGON TRAIL

A folk revival fully exploded in the late '50s and early '60s in urban centers and on college campuses around the country. A new generation of postwar "boomers" seeking an identity to separate themselves from 1950s conservatism had discovered authenticity in America's native sounds. It was essentially a continuation of the 1930s folk revival, which had been interrupted by war and a political backlash against the far-left strains of the earlier cultural movement, but this secondary revival gained momentum from the advance of mass media. Folk music really took off the day the Kingston Trio, a clean-cut group popular with college students, released the old ballad "Tom Dooley" in 1958. With the help of prime-time TV and the Billboard charts, the folk sound dominated the music scene for years, as this revival produced some of the most enduring folk artists of the twentieth century.

Woody Guthrie did not participate in the second revival, but he was its father figure. As early as the late 1940s, Guthrie began suffering from the same hereditary condition with which his mother had been diagnosed, Huntington's chorea. The degenerative nerve disease left him unable to control his motion, his speech, his memory, and his moods. Ralph Bennett, the BPA employee who'd escorted Woody around the NRECA conference in Spokane in 1947, later said that it was clear even then that Guthrie was exhibiting a change in demeanor. He suffered largely out of the public eye. He stopped performing. By the early 1950s, Guthrie was

Washington Square Park in the early '60s

too sick to record any music effectively. In the studio, he forgot words and chords. In fits of self-medication, he drank himself into either rages or stupors. He was eventually hospitalized for more than twelve years, a prisoner of his condition until he died in 1967.*

But in the man's absence, his legend only grew as his biography was subject to ever-greater mythmaking and hyperbole. His songs—from a singer who'd had no real commercial success, who didn't sell many records, and who in fact had rarely recorded—began to take on a life of their own. In England, a Scottish skiffle singer named Lonnie Donegan reached number six on the British charts with his version of "Grand Coulee Dam" in 1958. Between 1961 and 1964, twenty-seven artists released versions of "Pastures of Plenty." Woody's traveling partners Cisco Houston and Ramblin' Jack Elliott were also instrumental in spreading his songs.

Woody was like a ghost. His songs were being sung by fans who idolized him but really didn't know him. Some did come looking. In 1961, a young Minnesotan folksinger named Bob Zimmerman visited Guthrie in the hospital and shared some of his songs. Soon after the visit, he included "Song to Woody" on his first album, self-titled after his stage name: Bob Dylan.

In 1976, nine years after Guthrie's death, a biopic about him, *Bound for Glory*, was released (always confirmation of iconic status), and Guthrie's legend had peaked. He was no longer simply a folksinger who wrote

*Guthrie's erratic behavior in the early 1950s was mistakenly diagnosed as alcoholism and/or schizophrenia until 1952 when he was correctly diagnosed with Huntington's chorea, the incurable degenerative nerve disorder now known as Huntington's disease or HD. He was admitted to Greystone Park Psychiatric Hospital in 1954, and during the last decade of his life, Guthrie was a prisoner in his own body, unable to write and play yet, according to those near him, still mentally sharp and cognizant. He was visited by many of the new folk artists of the time, who paid homage to Woody and played songs for him. His second wife, Marjorie, and his family continued to visit and bring him home for weekends until he died on October 3, 1967, at Creedmoor State Hospital. Phillip Buehler's excellent *Woody Guthrie's Wardy Forty: Greystone Park State Hospital Revisited* chronicles these last years.

about the people. Critics were beginning to view him "as some western Chaucer," America's folk poet laureate, a seminal songster who showed a singular ability to capture the American experience in verse. But as Woody Guthrie's fame increased over the decades, the knowledge of his songwriting for the government seemed to run in the inverse. That's a bit surprising, since Guthrie himself wrote about it, it was the subject of an AP wire story in 1963, and Ramblin' Jack Elliott impersonated Guthrie saying "I wrote twenty-six songs in thirty days" on an intro to his version of "Talking Columbia." Joe Klein also briefly mentions Guthrie's work for the BPA in his definitive 1980 biography, *Woody Guthrie: A Life*.

However, the story had faded enough into obscurity that by 1979, one Pacific Northwest folksinger had no idea of the history of Guthrie on the Columbia River—nor did his supervisors at the BPA.

It was a damp day in Portland when thirty-eight-year-old Bill Murlin sat watching movies in the fourth-floor film library of the BPA's headquarters at 911 NE Eleventh Avenue.

Murlin spent most of his childhood in the Spokane valley. Then in 1959 he attended Washington State University in Pullman, to study broadcasting, where he got caught up in the folk craze sweeping the country. He and two other guys started a folk trio, which became a folk duo when one the members was accepted to law school. Murlin and Carl Allen called themselves the Wanderers. Being a resident of the region, Murlin was always curious about why folksingers sang so much about the Pacific Northwest. But it was an idle sort of curiosity—nothing to spur any serious investigation into the matter. After graduating, his family relocated to Salem, Oregon, and he kept playing folk music while holding a series of jobs at radio and television stations around the region, before being hired on by the BPA's public information office.

One of Murlin's jobs at the BPA was assisting at the film library, which loaned out movies the agency had gathered over its forty-plus-year history. As Murlin recalled, it was a surprisingly extensive collection. Among the titles produced by the agency were *Hydro, Power Builds*

Ships, and, of course, *The Columbia*. Out of curiosity, he started screening some of the sixteen-millimeter films. In the opening credits of *The Columbia*, he saw Guthrie's name. He nearly jumped out of his seat.

"I just didn't know much about Woody Guthrie's history at all, and I had no clue he'd been up in the Northwest," he recalled.

He did a little bit of digging and found a folder of production notes about *The Columbia* that included some of Guthrie's personnel papers. That was an even bigger surprise.

"Woody Guthrie worked here?" he remembered thinking in shock.

"Turns out, of course, that he's spent quite a lot of time out here, but I had to find that out for myself," Murlin said. "How long was he here? What did he do? How did he do it, and why, and so forth? And I started digging around to see what I could find within the confines of the Bonneville Power Administration."

The BPA's records were woefully incomplete. Beyond the personnel records, no evidence existed of Guthrie's actual work there, be it written lyrics or recordings of him singing his Columbia River songs. His boss was intrigued by Murlin's initial research enough, however, to allow him to travel to Seattle for three days to pull some files housed at the National Archives there, and to write to some Woody Guthrie experts to gain a better understanding of the agency's history with him. Among those he wrote was Richard Reuss,* a folklorist who had compiled the definitive collection of Guthrie's writings to that point.

---

*Reuss was one of the foremost Guthrie scholars, and he published *A Woody Guthrie Bibliography: 1912–1967* in 1968. A folklorist and historian, his 1971 dissertation "American Folklore and Left Wing Politics 1927–1957" was eventually published in 2000. He was primarily a collector and documenter who provided first-hand accounts of the folk revival as a participant in the 1960s via interviews, along with exhaustive note-taking at concerts and performances. He passed away in 1986 at age forty-six, shortly after making contact with Bill Murlin regarding Guthrie's Columbia songs. It's unclear if he ever heard Woody Guthrie singing "Roll On, Columbia" from the recording discovered by Murlin in 1985.

Reuss soon wrote back: "The songs Woody wrote for the BPA are indeed among his greatest, and also best known. Unlike other periods when he wrote batches of songs around a single theme or topic, almost every effort was a good if not outstanding composition."

Responding to Murlin's question as to whether a recording existed of Guthrie singing the most famous Columbia River song, Reuss suggested that it did not.

"Unfortunately, I can't help you with a recorded version of 'Roll On, Columbia' by Woody Guthrie. . . . Actually, it isn't too surprising; there are quite a few of his well-known songs which he personally didn't record (or at least they were not released)."

Reuss also provided Murlin with an invaluable document: a 1945 letter from the BPA to Bess Lomax Hawes, Alan's sister, who at the time worked for the Office of War Information. With it were twenty-four manuscripts of songs Guthrie wrote for the BPA. That letter—Reuss's copy may have been the last in existence, as neither the BPA nor Bess Lomax Hawes had retained copies of it—remains today as the most definitive proof of which songs Guthrie wrote while in Portland.

Thrilled by his fast progress, Murlin went to his supervisor with a proposition to make a new documentary about Guthrie's time at the agency—something that would "include part of this story, and include some of Woody Guthrie's music as part of the soundtrack," Murlin recalled. "And the bosses basically said, 'Nah, that's not part of your job. It's not a big deal. . . . Just put it aside.' So I did."

That could have been the end of Murlin's research, but in 1984 the BPA began making plans to celebrate its fiftieth anniversary, coming in 1987. Put on the committee to plan the celebration, Murlin saw the opportunity to pick up the trail again. He first suggested that the agency hire a Woody Guthrie look-alike to drive up and down the river singing Guthrie's songs. That idea was turned down, but an even more compelling one was suggested by Murlin: a twenty-six-song songbook that would represent the first-ever full compilation of all the music Guthrie wrote for the BPA.

Figuring out the details of Woody Guthrie's time at the BPA was challenging from the start. Among Guthrie's own archives, no detailed journals of his time in Portland survived—an anomaly for a person who constantly wrote down his experiences. Nor did he seem to have ever put the Columbia River song cycle into a songbook, also strange for Guthrie. At the BPA, poor record-keeping also left a lot of questions. Guthrie had repeatedly said he wrote twenty-six songs during his month in Portland, a figure that was confirmed by Kahn. However, the letter Reuss gave Murlin contained only twenty-four songs. That left two to be found—if Guthrie was to be believed on his twenty-six-song figure.

Bill Murlin, right, audiovisual specialist for the BPA, with Ramblin' Jack Elliott, left, during the BPA's fiftieth anniversary at Bonneville Dam, 1987

In search of answers, Murlin wrote an article in the BPA's employee newsletter asking workers and retirees who'd been around in 1941 if they had any information about Guthrie's tenure at the agency. That article found its way to the *Oregonian*, Portland's largest daily paper, which ran an article about Murlin's search on the front page of a Monday edition.

Murlin had hit a nerve. The response was immediate. The long-forgotten story of Woody Guthrie on the Columbia River was too good for news editors across the country to resist. Soon after the big splash in the local paper, interview requests from across the country inundated Murlin. Over three days, he appeared on CBS, NBC, ABC, and PBS. He was also interviewed by a German magazine.

"Sometimes I got hoarse answering the interviews, but I did them all," he said.

With his search for Guthrie material now national news, Murlin began receiving bits of information from across the country. Most of it wasn't very useful—people writing to say they had a studio version of some of the Grand Coulee Dam songs, for example. Then he got a letter from Ralph Bennett, who at that point was the managing editor at the *San Diego Tribune*, saying that he had some acetate copies of the original basement recordings Guthrie made at the BPA.

At Murlin's request, Bennett transferred his recordings onto a cassette tape and mailed it to him. Bennett also suggested that Murlin get hold of his friend Merle Meacham, for whom he'd made some copies. Meacham indeed still had them, and sent those to Murlin as well. Meanwhile, Gordon Macnab, now retired from reporting for AP, shared with Murlin a 33⅓ rpm record dubbed from three recordings he'd gotten directly from Kahn in the early 1960s when working on a story about Guthrie at the BPA.

Murlin could hardly believe what he had received: in search of information simply on what songs Guthrie had written, Murlin was suddenly listening to recordings that had long been considered lost.

Among them was something that Murlin recognized as a true prize for the Guthrie discography: the recording of Guthrie singing "Roll On, Columbia"—the recording that all Guthrie experts believed did not exist.

"It was just like manna dropping out of heaven," Murlin said. "It was just like digging in an old played-out gold mine and suddenly discovering a new vein."

In total, there were six discs containing a total of fourteen songs, two of which were duplicates.* On Macnab's 33⅓ rpm piece of vinyl, there were the three recordings used in *The Columbia*: "Biggest Thing That Man Has Ever Done," "Roll, Columbia, Roll," and the cherished minor-key modal version of "Pastures of Plenty"—which in the movie had been cut into three parts in order to fit the script. This full-length version was a revelation.

Meacham supplied "Jackhammer Blues," "The Song of the Grand Coulee Dam" (a.k.a. "Way Up in That Northwest), "Columbia Waters" (a.k.a. "Good Morning, Mr. Captain"), and "Columbia Talking Blues."

Bennett supplied a demo version of "Biggest Thing That Man Has Ever Done," "Washington Talkin' Blues," "Ramblin' Blues" (a.k.a. "Portland Town"), "Grand Coulee Dam," "Roll On, Columbia," "It Takes a Married Man" and a different version of "The Song of the Grand Coulee Dam."

It was a good thing Murlin got the "Roll On, Columbia" recording when he did. Bennett had often thought about getting rid of the old acetate discs, and had done very little to preserve them over the years. When Murlin learned of their existence, he flew to San Diego to retrieve the originals. He was so concerned with preserving them—especially the recording of Guthrie singing one of his most famous songs—that he had a special box made that kept the discs separated from each other to preserve their quality. In later research, Bill Murlin learned that Guthrie did try to record "Roll On, Columbia" in the 1950s, but by that time he was too sick to remember the lyrics or record effectively. Thus, the surviving studio demo is not considered a part of the Woody Guthrie discography.

Murlin estimates that the time between the *Oregonian* article appearing and his having all the recordings in hand was less than a year.

*The six discs with the names of the donors are housed in the National Archives in Washington, DC, and represent twelve unique Woody Guthrie recordings not heard before. Of the twelve recordings, six of them were Guthrie songs never heard before and six were songs recorded either by Woody himself, or others, after his 1941 BPA experience. The 1987 Rounder album *The Columbia River Collection* represents eleven of these twelve recordings—"Pastures of Plenty" was considered too poor in sound quality to be included on the collection, but does appear on Rounder's 2013 release *American Radical Patriot*.

He immediately recognized that he had more than just the makings of a nice songbook for the BPA, but an album made up largely of never-before-heard Guthrie material. The BPA quickly agreed to underwrite a record for its fiftieth anniversary.

Murlin and his bosses made the assumption that since Guthrie wrote the songs while employed by the federal government, the songs were in the public domain. In fact, the question of who owned the Columbia River songs had never been explored: Woody, a consummate folksinger, never concerned himself with licensing or copyrights. He had freely used the songs for the rest of his career, and the BPA had never objected.

But from the BPA's standpoint, the documents clearly showed that he produced them at taxpayers' expense, so the public should not have to pay again, for the song rights.

The Guthrie estate didn't agree. As Woody Guthrie's stature grew over the decades, his management and heirs became stalwarts for their father's legacy. They not only wanted copyright control over all of his songs, but they didn't want his music used for any commercial purposes that the singer wouldn't have believed in. Were the Columbia River songs to enter the public domain, every chamber of commerce and bank in the country could conceivably use his songs in their marketing.

Staring down the road to a lawsuit—which both sides feared would reflect poorly on them—they struck an agreement. The songs would remain the property of the Guthrie estate, and the BPA could use them for the princely sum of one dollar.

With Murlin's discoveries, there were now a total of seventeen Columbia River songs recorded by Guthrie known to be in existence. When putting together his record, Murlin wanted to use as many of the newly discovered versions as possible. But that proved to be impossible in the case of "Pastures of Plenty," which had lost a great deal of quality when dubbed. All told, the BPA released twelve never-before-provided Guthrie recordings, supplemented with five commercial recordings Guthrie made with Moe Asch in New York after leaving Portland.

Meanwhile, Murlin was still putting together the songbook.

While the recordings had incalculable value, they did not help in Murlin's quest to find the missing songs. In consultation with Guthrie experts including Pete Seeger, Murlin determined that the never-recorded song "Grand Coulee Powder Monkey" (found in the songbook *The Nearly Complete Collection of Woody Guthrie Folk Songs*) must have been written by Guthrie while at the BPA. Another one, "New Found Land," touches on many of the same themes of a "planned promised land" that informed other Columbia River

The BPA Songbook, 1988

songs and appeared on Moe Asch's first collection of Guthrie Columbia River songs (that curiously titled *Ballads from the Dust Bowl*). Because of that information, Murlin felt comfortable including "New Found Land" in his tally.

It is important to emphasize that no evidence has been found to directly tie these two songs to Guthrie's BPA employment, a frustrating fact for historical completists. However, given the fact that Guthrie repeatedly cited the twenty-six figure, and the fact that all of these songs clearly deal with Columbia River subjects, Murlin's conclusion has never been questioned.

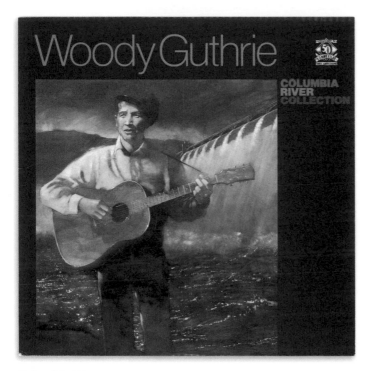

Columbia River
Collection *album
cover, Rounder
Records, 1987*

The next challenge for the songbook was that there were five songs in which only the lyrics survived—with no melody to accompany them. The songs were "Lumber Is King," "Guys on the Grand Coulee Dam," "Portland Town to Klamath," "White Ghost Train," and "Ballad of Jackhammer John." On account of the tradition of folk music, this wasn't as big of a problem as it may seem: Guthrie modeled many of his Columbia River songs on existing folk melodies, and Murlin surmised that someone with a sharp ear for traditional songs could identify which tune he had in mind when he wrote the remaining lyrics. The sharp ear Murlin decided to enlist was that of Seeger.

Seeger proved to be a very willing participant, and he figured out most of the folk melodies. For example, he determined that "Guys on the Grand Coulee Dam" fit the tune of "Widdicombe Fair"; "White Ghost Train" used "Wabash Cannonball"; "Portland Town to Klamath" was based on "Crawdad Song"; and "The Ballad of Jackhammer John" adapted "House of the Rising Sun." However, Seeger was stumped by "Lumber Is King," so in classic folk tradition, he wrote a new melody himself. More than forty years after Seeger and Guthrie met at the Forrest Theatre, the two were still collaborating on music.

The album of seventeen recordings was released by Rounder Records as the *Columbia River Collection* in 1987 on the day of the BPA's fiftieth anniversary. The songbook, *Roll On Columbia: The Columbia River Songs*—delayed on account of a tardy yet fantastically extensive introduction written by Alan Lomax—came out later in 1988.

But that wasn't the end of Murlin's journey.

Throughout the process, he was bothered by how little information remained in BPA files about Guthrie. Recordings, photographs, raw footage, and paperwork all seemed to have disappeared. "The government doesn't throw anything away," Murlin remarked.*

One explanation for this came by way of an incredible story told to him by Elmer Buehler, the man who'd driven Guthrie around during his month on the Columbia.

In the late 1940s, anti-public-power Republicans in Washington slashed the BPA's budget, which caused Buehler to lose his job. Because of his tenure, he was able to take a new job in the organization if he so chose, and he decided to go to work in its maintenance-and-gardening department. One of the duties this new position carried was operation of the BPA's incinerator in Vancouver, Washington. For the rest of his life, Buehler asserted that in the early 1950s—under the Eisenhower administration, which had installed former Oregon governor and public-power foe Douglas McKay as secretary of the interior—orders came down to destroy material related to public-power advocacy, including the movie *The Columbia*. Buehler insists that he was given nitrate film to burn in the incinerator.

"We were told to burn it," Buehler said under oath. "Well, I had just been in the Army, and I took my orders from people above me, of course, and I always did in the government but I said I'm not going to destroy this nitro film, because it will blow up the incinerator."

He was told to burn the film anyway, and said he burned a total of twenty-five copies of *The Columbia* and its predecessor, *Hydro*.

---

* The government actually does dispose of records, employment papers, and other materials in accordance to the Code of Federal Regulations (CFR). Thus records are appraised and then disposed of—or kept—regularly, depending on the determination of their permanent value.

However, in fear of losing the Guthrie material forever, he secreted a couple of copies away.

"I hid them in the basement behind a woodpile and I didn't even dare talk to anybody about it," he said. "Figured that I'd be crucified."

It wasn't until the 1970s that Buehler handed his copies over to an Oklahoma film historian named Harry Menig, who wanted to screen the film.

"I can't write a book, but I sure can save a film," he later said.

Murlin investigated Buehler's claim, conducting interviews with everyone still alive in the 1980s who may have known about an anti-public-power purge at the BPA. No one corroborated nor refuted Buehler's claim, though several expressed generally negative opinions about Woody Guthrie's work at the agency.

A 1980 investigation into the claims by the BPA administrator concluded that Buehler's story "has remained consistent over a significant number of years and has never been refuted. It is part of the official records in the National Archives in Washington, D.C., and appears destined to become a permanent part of the BPA's history, though it may never be verified by other witnesses."

It is conceivable that a purge during the height of the Cold War—which included blacklisting in other sections of the government, media, and the entertainment industry—could have taken place at the BPA. Many of the New Dealers, including Kahn, did not stay beyond 1950, and many of the public-utility efforts were becoming private-public partnerships under the new administration. But if true, it was most likely a minor effort, since copies of *The Columbia* still existed in schools, stock houses, and movie theater archives.

Still, whether intentional purge or simply carelessness, the loss of recordings and work by Woody Guthrie at the BPA leaves a regrettable hole in our current understanding of his time in the Northwest. Among the material lost forever seems to be the raw footage of *The Columbia*, the original basement recordings Guthrie made at the BPA, and the original recordings that Kahn made of Guthrie in New York for the movie's soundtrack.

The holes might have been even larger if it weren't for a final, dramatic act by Murlin in his quest to resurrect the story of Guthrie at the BPA. In 1991, Murlin discovered that federal law required that employee records be retained for fifty years after their term of employment, and 1991 marked fifty years for Guthrie. So he renewed his search for the folksinger's employment records and was told that anything about him would have been sent to a central repository in Saint Louis, Missouri. Calling the National Archives office there, he was told they did indeed have the file.

"The people in Saint Louis said, 'Oh, yeah, it's here. It's on our conveyor belt headed for the shredder,'" Murlin recalled. "I said, 'Get that thing off the conveyor belt, now!' So they did."

The fiftieth anniversary of Guthrie's time at the BPA prompted another series of news articles about the event—greatly elucidated by Murlin's research. The recovered acetate recordings of Meacham, Macnab, and Bennett were inducted into the National Archives in 1987.

Speaking to the *New York Times* in 1991, Stephen Kahn reflected on the contributions that Guthrie made to the BPA during his one month with the agency. All things considered, he noted, "I don't think the Government has ever gotten a better investment on its money."

COLUMBIA TALKING BLUES
(By Woody Guthrie)

Down along the river just a settin on a rock
Lookin at the boats in the Bonneville lock;
  Gate swings open, and the boat sails in;
  She toots her whistle, and she's gone again.
              Gasoline a going up. Wheat a coming down.

Lot of folks around the country, politicians and such,
Said the old Columbia wouldn't never 'mount to much;
  Times a coming, and it wont be long,
  Till you're a gonna see that there's somebody wrong.
              Thousand years. All this here water just a going to waste.

Filled up my hat brim, drunk a little taste,
Thought about a river just a going to waste;
  Thought about the Dust, thought about the Sand,
  Thought about the people, thought about the land.
              Folks a running around. Lookin for a little place.

Fellers back east they done a lot of talking,
Some of them a balking, some of them a squaking;
  But with all their figures, with all their books,
  Them boys didn't know their Royal Chinooks.
              Good river. Needs some more big dams on it.

Well, I pulled out my pencil and I scribbled this song,
Figured all of them Salmon just couldn't be wrong;
  Them salmon fish is pretty shrewd,
  They got senators and politicians, too.
              Just like a president. Run every four years.

You just watch this river, and pretty soon
Everybody's a gong to change their tune;
  The big Grand Coulee, and the Bonneville Dam,
  Run a thousand factories for Uncle Sam.
              Everything from fertilizer to bombing planes.

Uncle Sam needs houses, and stuff to eat,
Uncle Sam needs wool, Uncle Sam needs wheat;
  Uncle Sam needs water and power dams,
  Uncle Sam needs people, and the people need land.
              Dont like Dictators. But the whole country'd ought to
              be run by Electricity.

CHAPTER 9

TALKIN' COLUMBIA

Why are the songs so great? Look through his songbooks. The songs are honest. But above all else, Woody's songs show the genius of simplicity. Any damn fool can get complicated, but it takes a genius to attain simplicity. Some of his greatest songs are so deceptively simple that your eye will pass right over them and you will comment to yourself, 'Well, I guess this was one of his lesser efforts.' Years later you will find the song has grown on you and become part of your life.

—PETE SEEGER

oday, the twenty-six songs Woody Guthrie wrote for Bonneville remain an accomplishment in terms of songwriting, but they ultimately stand the test of time as one of Woody's finest bodies of work—a song cycle that was unusually focused and extremely inspiring. There's no doubt that "Pastures of Plenty," "Grand Coulee Dam," and "Roll On, Columbia" have outlived their usefulness in promoting the Columbia River projects, but they live on in the pantheon of American folk music.

The Columbia River songs have appreciated in time in another way as well. It is our assertion that the twenty-six songs are a direct response to Woody's earlier, and much more celebrated, Dust Bowl ballads. In their optimism, the songs reflect the hope of a nation emerging from a decade of hard times, environmental calamity, and displacement by embracing bold public works projects and the idea of tangibly helping common people. In his Columbia River songs, he conveyed a sense that something better was coming, that the "planned promised land" in the Pacific Northwest was indeed a solution to the Dust Bowl crisis.

"We're talking about a certain time in American history—the Depression, hard times, coming out of it a bit, but not quite solvent," said Studs Terkel, the Chicago writer and Woody's friend. "But at the same time there was a kinda optimistic spirit, like a light at the end of the tunnel, you felt something popping . . . and Woody caught that spirit!"

But hanging over the legacy of Woody Guthrie's month of writing hopeful songs about the "planned promised land" in Oregon and Washington is a simple fact: it never truly came to be.

As planners envisioned it, and as Guthrie put to song, the Grand Coulee Dam would irrigate a wide network of small farms and provide work and sustenance to the farmers who lost their land in the Dust Bowl. However, World War II had a profound effect on these dreams. The war permanently altered America's economy to the urban, industrial one we know today. It also delayed the construction of the irrigation project for more than a decade, as efforts went completely toward producing power for the war.

It wasn't until 1951 that water began to be pumped from the Lake Roosevelt reservoir behind Grand Coulee Dam. Though not at the scale once hoped for, today the Columbia Basin Project irrigates 670,000 acres of land and drives a $630 million agriculture industry.

However, it is not for the benefit of Dust Bowl refugees that the water flows.

After World War I, the question had been asked about returning US soldiers: "How do you expect to keep them down on the farm after they've seen Paris?" After World War II, the question seemed all the more pertinent. So in the late 1940s, the Bureau of Reclamation mapped out forty-one thousand acres of small farms on land it had purchased to help bring farmers into the area—with preference given to war veterans.

While interest in the plots was initially high, many prospective farmers quickly backed out of plans to farm the new land.

The challenge of drawing farmers to the area became painfully clear to the Bureau of Reclamation with a publicity stunt to promote the program.

The Farm-in-a-Day demonstration project in 1952 was meant to show the kind of transformation that irrigation could bring to an area. A World War II veteran named Donald Dunn was awarded a new $50,000 farm, free of charge, in Moses Lake, Washington, and in twenty-four hours, volunteers constructed a house and tilled and irrigated the land. Dunn seemed like the perfect recipient. His farm in Kansas had been destroyed in a flood the year before, and he was considered a "top-notch farmer." He had great success in Moses Lake, especially with potatoes, but within four years, he had sold the land to try his luck elsewhere,

Apple Blossom Queens pouring water from all fifty states into the Grand Coulee's main irrigation canal for the 1951 inaugural ceremony

Columbia Basin farming with Grand Coulee water, circa 1960s

saying that lack of a market and restrictions put on him in Washington State were too much.

Most of the farmers who bought land in the newly irrigated area were from the Pacific Northwest already, meaning that no serious relocation occurred. Meanwhile, attempts by the government to create new townsites in the irrigation district were flops. One Washington town, called Burke, was outright rejected, because nearby towns feared it would divert business from their shops. Another, George, still exists today but is hardly a shining example of a twentieth-century planned community.

Over the decades, the government eased restrictions on how small farms had to be to take advantage of Columbia River projects, and larger agribusinesses moved onto the land. Today, Grant County, Washington, in the heart of the area, proudly touts itself on green highway signs as the number one potato-producing county in the country. As Oregon historian Paul Pitzer put it, the irrigation project as envisioned by New Dealers was "a nineteenth-century plan for a twentieth-century economy."

The spread of publicly owned power kept closer to its original vision. Throughout the Northwest, PUDs and municipal power systems continue to supply millions of homes with electricity. Many towns today hang highway signs telling travelers that they are "Another Public Power Community," and the region as a whole boasts more publicly owned utilities than any other in the nation. The area has also enjoyed over the last seventy-five years some of the cheapest power rates in the country, just as Roosevelt had all but promised it would when promoting the dam projects.

Ironically, for all the talk in the 1930s of the Columbia River projects creating a new agrarian society, the dams' most enduring legacy may be the large urban centers of the Pacific Northwest: Seattle and Portland. Following World War II, both cities continued to flex their industrial might in peacetime, running on power from the dams. Continued damming of the river also all but eliminated flood risk in Portland—just as Kahn had said it would in *The Columbia*—allowing that metropolis to flourish. Indeed, it's hard to imagine the cities as they are today without the benefits of the dams.

"These great dams of the west are why we have the metropolitan areas of the West," said historian Margaret O'Mara.

Even the cheap electricity, though, carries its own complicated coda.

For one, it played an instrumental role in the development of nuclear weapons. In 1943, unbeknownst to the public, power from the Grand Coulee Dam began to be transmitted to a secret compound in Central Washington that was enriching plutonium to be used in the atomic bomb dropped on Nagasaki. Today, the Hanford Site is one of the biggest and most complex environmental-cleanup projects in the country.

Meanwhile, many of those people most impacted by the Grand Coulee Dam never saw the full benefits they were promised. The tribes

The first water from the Grand Coulee Dam pours into the Columbia Basin canal system, 1951

whose land was flooded and whose lifestyle was forever altered by the dam went uncompensated for their losses for sixty-one years, until 1994 when a federal court ordered that the Confederated Tribes of the Colville Reservation be paid $53 million in compensation.

"For years, they didn't have phone service," Blaine Harden, author of *A River Lost,* said of the Colville tribes. "They didn't get the cheap electricity that white people . . . got. They were really, really dispossessed of everything and were always an afterthought."

The salmon runs on the Columbia today—which Guthrie marveled at during his time here—have been decimated, though dams do not carry sole blame for that fact. Millions of dollars are now being spent to restore salmon runs across the region through hatchery programs and habitat protection, but all species of salmon are listed as either threatened or endangered in at least one part of the Columbia Basin.

The people paid for advocating the Columbia River projects—Stephen Kahn, Ralph Bennett, and Michael Loring, who worked with Woody Guthrie at the BPA—all suggested a change in the wind when the Eisenhower administration ushered a free-market ideology into the federal government. This isn't to suggest that the cause of their marginalization was working with Guthrie, but rather their shared belief in an activist government agency.

They weren't the only Guthrie contemporaries to face a backlash as the Red Scare swept the country. Alan Lomax, who got Guthrie his job with the BPA, was investigated for communist ties, and decided to take a job in Europe for most of the 1950s. Pete Seeger was blacklisted due to his ties to communism and did not appear on commercial television until 1967. Guthrie himself was investigated by the FBI, but was so sick by the mid-1950s that he wasn't considered a threat to the nation.

Given this complicated history, it's fair to ask whether Woody Guthrie's Columbia River songs are anything but relics of a time never come. While it's difficult to assign value to any piece of art, the endurance of Woody Guthrie's Columbia River songs seems to suggest that they do have worth in the twenty-first century.

Though the full designs of the Columbia River projects never came to be, as dreamed they represented a radical proposition for the nation—a vision of an engineered society in which the worker, Roosevelt's "forgotten man," is put first.

Seventy-five years after his Portland experience, Woody Guthrie stands secure in his embodiment of American folk identity. His songs represent the character of a great generation, the hard times they overcame, and the spirit of a social democracy.

To what extent the "planned promised land" succeeded or failed cannot diminish the idealism of Woody Guthrie's songs and his vision for a better place in which the bounty of resources were shared by all, "cuz our pastures of plenty must always be free."

Special busses bring tourists
to the Grand Coulee Dam, Wash.

© 1947
WESTERN
SOUVENIRS
322

ACKNOWLEDGMENTS

I first came upon the story of Woody Guthrie's Columbia River songs when visiting the Grand Coulee Dam's visitor center and hearing an unidentified version of "Roll On, Columbia" full of female harmony and '80s spirit. The question of how many other versions of the song existed led me on a quest, and soon to the entire song cycle. In 2008, I produced and aired a three-hour radio special on KEXP-FM Seattle about this local history.

The long road from radio special to book involves many people to whom I'm indebted.

Michael Madjic's documentary *Roll On, Columbia* from the University of Oregon was the basis of my radio special. I updated the original 2008 broadcast during Guthrie's centennial in 2012, which caught the ear of my publisher, Gary Luke at Susquatch Books. He and vice president and associate publisher (and KEXP fan) Sarah Hanson took a chance on this first-time author and championed the project from the beginning. I'd also like to thank Anna Goldstein for the beautiful design and Em Gale for keeping things straight during the many edits and confusing details.

The book became a reality thanks to the deft hand of my cowriter, Dan Person. His ability to complete my thoughts and theories, flesh out the writing, and assist in the research (the Popular Front!) was essential.

Many people assisted me during my research. First and foremost, the enthusiastic Libby Burke, archivist at the Bonneville Power Administration Library in Portland, Oregon, who was always there to answer my questions (not many know more about this story than

Libby). Also the entire BPA Library staff was generous, including Tina L. Kay for her photo archival research.

The Woody Guthrie Center and Archives in Tulsa, Oklahoma, hosted me for a week. Archivist Kate Blalack was patient and helpful with this first-time researcher, and Deana McCloud and her staff took me to lunch every day. Anna Canoni of Woody Guthrie Publications kept me sane during many moments of high anxiety.

Jon Kertzer invited me to present this story at his "Woody at 100: The Guthrie Legacy Conference" in Edmonton, Alberta, in 2012 and worked his magic in negotiating the publishing rights for Woody's Columbia River song manuscripts that appear in this book.

Lynne Brougher and staff at the Bureau of Land Reclamation at the Grand Coulee Dam were helpful with photo requests, as well as David Walsh at the Boise, Idaho, office. Scott Hunter from the *Star* in Grand Coulee went above and beyond the call of duty in helping me when he really didn't have to.

I relied on the knowledge and kindness of many others: Jeff Place and Stephanie Smith of Smithsonian Folkways, Todd Harvey of the American Folklife Center at the Library of Congress, Nathan Salsburg of the Alan Lomax Archive, and Bob Santelli of the GRAMMY Museum. Also generous were Guy Logsden, Paul Pitzer, Michael Kazan, Bill Nowlin, Mark Loring, Ellen Geer, Barry Ollman, Karen Kahn, and Ed Cray for his book *Ramblin' Man*, which we used for much of our source material.

Many thanks and gratitude goes to Bill Murlin, who was a key resource for me from the radio-show beginning. He contributed mightily when I needed the real nitty-gritty in terms of the very confusing matrix of Woody's Columbia River songs. Joe Seamons also supplied support in the early days of this project as only a true itinerant folksinger/educator can. And thanks to Hobe Kytr, the fisher poet.

I'd also like to acknowledge the many friends and colleagues who did me right when I needed them over the past eighteen months—my KEXP peeps: John Richards, Kevin Cole, Cheryl Waters, Dylan Flesch, Will "Chilly" Myers, and Hans Fluegel. Katie McKenna, Sean Jewell, Robynne Hawthorne, Scott Giampino, Victoria VanBruinesse, Chris Estey, Pat Thomas, Paul and Melissa Vandegrift, Coco Foto, and Gabe Johnson helped me in various ways. A special thanks goes to Drew Christie for being amazing and Jeff Jewell for the very early inspiration.

And a posthumous thanks to Steve Kahn and Elmer Buehler. May you both rest in peace.

Electricity and all

I love a longshoreman, I do mama,
I love a longshoreman, I do, ha ha,
We're gonna get married, we are, mama,
And have electricity and all.

He held my hand, he did, mama,
He held my hand, he did, ha ha,
We're gonna have ~~have~~ children around our door
and have electricity and all.

We walked on the sea shore, we did, mama,
We walked on the sea shore, we did, ha ha,
He whispered and told me the way it would be
to have electricity and all.

He combed my hair, he did, mama,
He combed my hair, he did, ha ha,
He said it would wave when we get settled down
and have electricity and all.

He hugged me tight, he did, mama,
He hugged me tight, he did, ha ha,
He said he would hug me morning and night
when we have electricity and all.

He kissed my lips, he did, mama,
He kissed my lips, he did, ha ha,
He said that he'd kiss me a million times
when we get electricity and all.

I'm going to tell papa, I am, mama,
I'm going to tell papa, I am, ha ha —
He might not like it but I don't care
'Cause we'll have electricity and all.

Woody Guthrie

WG-1-03-10-A

DISCOGRAPHY

Roll On, Columbia

One of the first songs Woody Guthrie wrote upon arriving in Portland in May of 1941, it's the defining ballad in his Columbia River song cycle. He briefed himself on the area even before arriving by reading road maps and pamphlets representing a "cardboard history" of the Northwest. Once hired, Guthrie was provided reading materials including a book on the history of the local "Indian wars," featuring a US Army general named Phil Sheridan. Over time, Guthrie edited out racially insensitive caricatures and politically incorrect references in the song that also commemorates Memaloose Island, a sacred Native American burial site. The use of "Good Night Irene" is an example of Guthrie's ability to repurpose familiar melodies in entirely new ways. An anthem to public power and named the official Washington State folk song in 1987, it has become one of Guthrie's most recognizable songs.

ORIGINAL TITLE: "Roll On Columbia, Roll On"

MELODY: "Good Night Irene"

RECORDINGS: 1941 BPA acetate copy recovered; available on the *Columbia River Collection* (Rounder, 1987); never recorded commercially by Guthrie

Biggest Thing That Man Has Ever Done

One of the three songs chosen for *The Columbia* soundtrack—an old ballad tracing back to 1894, first as "I'm a Highly Educated Man" and later as "I Was Born Ten Thousand Years Ago." Guthrie adapted it several times, calling it "The Great Historical Bum" and then "Biggest Thing That Man Has Ever Done" in order to describe the mammoth Grand Coulee Dam project for the Bonneville Power Administration. Jeff Place of Smithsonian Folkways said, "This song provided a perfect frame for Guthrie to hang his political commentary on."

MELODY: "Son of a Gambolier"

RECORDINGS: The 1942 soundtrack version recorded at Reeves Sound Studio in New York City is lost; a 1941 BPA acetate copy was recovered in the '80s, and that version is available on the *Columbia River Collection* (Rounder, 1987); also recorded commercially for Moe Asch on April 19, 1944, with Cisco Houston

Hard Travelin'

This song was written in 1940 at the apartment of Harold Ambellan and Elizabeth Higgins at 31 East Twenty-First Street in New York City's Flatiron District and later submitted to the BPA. Considered a Columbia River song although it has no mention of dams, irrigation, or electricity, Woody clearly used it to meet his song-a-day requirement. One of the most recorded songs in Woody's catalogue, it was a favorite during the folk revival of the early '60s. The song title also became a phrase in the folk lexicon to separate folksingers who had lived it, like Woody, and the new urban folksingers who hadn't.

MELODY: "This Train Is Bound for Glory" variant, but considered original

RECORDINGS: Not recorded by the BPA in any form; recorded commercially for Moe Asch on April 20, 1944, with Sonny Terry, and again in 1947; the later version appeared on *Ballads from the Dust Bowl* (Disc, 1947) and later on the *Columbia River Collection* (Rounder, 1987)

Grand Coulee Dam

One of the most popular songs in the song cycle, it contains perhaps Woody's most poetic line: "In the misty crystal glitter of that wild and wind ward spray." The song not only suggests the passion Woody found in the landscape but also his awe at the sheer size and scope of the Columbia River projects and the dam itself. The tune is "Wabash Cannonball," a particular favorite melody of Guthrie who used it in three Columbia River songs. Lonnie Donegan recorded "Grand Coulee Dam" in 1958, which peaked at number six on the UK charts, helping to ignite the folk revival there.

ORIGINAL TITLE: "Ballad of the Great Grand Coulee"

MELODY: "Wabash Cannonball"

RECORDINGS: 1941 BPA acetate copy recovered; available on the *Columbia River Collection* (Rounder, 1987); recorded commercially for Moe Asch with Cisco Houston in New York on April 19, 1944

Jackhammer Blues

Guthrie wrote his first "Jackhammer Blues" in 1940 while observing jackhammering outside his New York City hotel room, as he cites in the BPA manuscript. That song, which imitates the sound of a jackhammer and was never recorded (it appears in *The Nearly Complete Collection of Woody Guthrie Songs*), is a completely different song than this Columbia River version, which he later recorded commercially for Moe Asch and renamed "Jackhammer John." This song is an ode to the hard work and rough-and-tumble lifestyle of the men who built the dams.

MELODY: "Brown's Ferry Blues"

RECORDINGS: 1941 BPA acetate copy recovered; available on the *Columbia River Collection* (Rounder, 1987); recorded commercially for Moe Asch as "Jackhammer John" on May 19, 1944; not to be confused with an earlier "Jackhammer Blues," written in 1940 but never recorded, or "The Ballad of Jackhammer John," another Columbia River song never recorded

Pastures of Plenty

"Pastures of Plenty" is one of Guthrie's most celebrated songs and one of the greatest folk songs ever written. It's a ballad about migrant workers and the promise of turning unusable land into an agricultural bread basket in the Columbia Basin. A direct response and/or answer to his earlier Dust Bowl ballads, this song was recorded along with two other Columbia River songs for *The Columbia* film soundtrack in New York in 1942. The minor key Guthrie used in this setting added greatly to the stark nature of the scenes of drought-stricken Dust Bowlers. The later and more familiar version Guthrie recorded with Moe Asch in a major key features a slightly up-tempo rhythm and harmonica, which dramatically changes the tone of the song from a "brooding melody" capturing the melancholy of the migrant dilemma into a more positive tune about the hope of irrigation for Dust Bowl refugees. One of the most popular compositions in the Guthrie catalog, it remains as one of the most frequently recorded Columbia River songs and continues to stand as an enduring anthem for social change.

MELODY: "Pretty Polly"

RECORDINGS: The original "modal" minor-key soundtrack version, recorded in 1942 at Reeves Sound Studio in New York City for the film *The Columbia*, is lost; a copy was found in the mid-1980s on a duplication record pressed in Portland, Oregon, by Gordon Macnab in the early 1960s and is included on *American Radical Patriot* (Rounder, 2013); recorded commercially in a major key for Moe Asch in New York City in 1947, and appeared on *Ballads from the Dust Bowl* (Disc, 1947) and the *Columbia River Collection* (Rounder, 1987)

Washington Talkin' Blues

This was one of the great discoveries of Bill Murlin's research in the 1980s. While many of Guthrie's 1941 river songs were recorded later in New York, this one was not. It's one of his best "talking blues," a form in which he was particularly skilled. Another direct response to his Dust Bowl ballads, this song is a blow-by-blow account of a Dust Bowl wheat farmer who moves to the Pacific Northwest before irrigation of the Columbia Basin, only to find the same conditions that he'd left behind. Guthrie adds to the lofty rhetoric of the New Deal with imagery of a brighter future and better opportunity from government intervention and a social democracy.

STYLE: Talking Blues

RECORDINGS: 1941 BPA acetate copy recovered; available on the *Columbia River Collection* (Rounder, 1987); never recorded commercially

Roll, Columbia, Roll

One of three songs recorded for *The Columbia* soundtrack, "Roll, Columbia, Roll" is featured in the opening scene of the film and plays like a love letter to the Pacific Northwest, with imagery that illuminates Guthrie's appreciation for the area's virgin landscape. It's a mix of Manifest Destiny and an unfortunate prevailing attitude that nature was begging to be conquered. Like the other songs used in the film's soundtrack, this recording surfaced on a vinyl copy pressed at Portland's Clair Recordings in the '60s, and it was discovered by Bill Murlin in the '80s. The duplicating process resulted in very poor fidelity, similar to the minor-key version of "Pastures of Plenty," which was on the same record copy.

MELODY: "Wabash Cannonball" variant but considered original

RECORDINGS: The original 1942 soundtrack version recorded at Reeves Sound Studio in New York City for the film *The Columbia* is lost; the copy found in the 1980s is available on the *Columbia River Collection* (Rounder, 1987)

Oregon Trail

The Pacific Northwest has long represented the land of promise, and this song is another optimistic response to Guthrie's earlier Dust Bowl ballads. It reinforces his belief in a brighter future without "bony" horses with ribs "you can count" and "cacklin'" chickens that lay "flint rock eggs." It's one of the better songs in the song cycle featuring a melody similar to that of "Hard Travelin'" in that it's as near to original as Woody would get.

ORIGINAL TITLE: "I'm A Gonna Hit That Oregon Line This Comin' Fall"

MELODY: Original

RECORDINGS: Not recorded by the BPA in any form; recorded commercially for Moe Asch in 1947 and appeared on *This Land Is Your Land* (Smithsonian Folkways, 1967) and the *Columbia River Collection* (Rounder, 1987)

Columbia Talkin' Blues

One of Guthrie's most frequently recorded songs, particularly by protégé Ramblin' Jack Elliott, it extolls the benefits of the dam projects while refuting criticism from eastern politicians, who "didn't know them raw Chinooks" (salmon) and suggests that the project was a white elephant. During the BPA recording, Woody ad-libbed the line "electricity running all around, cheaper than rainwater," which does not appear in the BPA manuscript. It was typical of Guthrie to not follow the script and to never perform a song the same way twice, like most folksingers.

ALTERNATE TITLE: "Talking Columbia"

STYLE: Talking Blues

RECORDINGS: 1941 BPA acetate copy recovered; available on the *Columbia River Collection* (Rounder, 1987); recorded commercially for Moe Asch in 1947 and appeared on *Ballads from the Dust Bowl* (Disc, 1947)

Ramblin' Blues

This song highlights the Bonneville Dam, forty miles upriver from Portland, and features an unemployed worker from Louisiana looking for a job on the project. Guthrie displays good local knowledge of Columbia's tributaries and relates the benefit of hydropower in the buildup to World War II.

The melody is from Blind Lemon Jefferson's "One Dime Blues." It's one of Guthrie's less original adaptations, suggesting the influence of Lead Belly on Guthrie's song writing. Guthrie would record the song again in 1944 and call it "New York Town" with obvious adaptations.

ALTERNATE TITLE: "Portland Town"

MELODY: "One Dime Blues"

RECORDINGS: 1941 BPA acetate copy recovered; available on the *Columbia River Collection* (Rounder, 1987); recorded commercially for Moe Asch as "New York Town" on April 19, 1944

Columbia Waters

Another previously unheard acetate recording discovered during Bill Murlin's research in the 1980s. Never recorded commercially, this song imagines a job seeker at the Grand Coulee Dam site introducing himself to a foreman—"Good morning, Mr. Captain!" Additional migrant imagery reinforces the idea that unemployed men and women really did want to work, but jobs were few. It's verification that a good job, government intervention, and settling down can help a family grow on the clean mountain water of the Pacific Northwest. Woody's patriotism is on display with the mention of Uncle Sam.

ALTERNATE TITLE: "Good Morning, Mr. Captain"

MELODY: "Muleskinner Blues"

RECORDINGS: 1941 BPA acetate copy recovered; available on the *Columbia River Collection* (Rounder, 1987); never recorded commercially

Ramblin' Round

This song was likely written prior to Woody's BPA experience. Guthrie describes the destitute situation of the unemployed during the Great Depression and the plight of Dust Bowl refugees who were forced to migrate and "go ramblin' 'round" looking for work. There's mention of the New Deal agricultural strategy of the 1930s to pay farmers not to harvest in order to stabilize prices. The melody is another adaptation on Lead Belly's "Good Night Irene." Sometimes Guthrie repurposed bits and pieces of music unconsciously, as is historically the case for many folk and blues artists.

MELODY: "Good Night Irene"

RECORDINGS: Not recorded for the BPA in any form; recorded commercially for Moe Asch in 1947; appeared on *Ballads from the Dust Bowl* (Disc, 1947), although titled "Ramblin' Blues" on the album; the same version also appears on the *Columbia River Collection* (Rounder, 1987)

End of My Line

This song describes the predicament of farmers who were not tied into the existing private power grid in the 1930s, before the hydroelectric projects on the Columbia River. While urban residents enjoyed a modern lifestyle that electricity provided, many rural people lived in the dark. A key component of the "planned promised land" was to bring convenience to every home, providing electricity and irrigation for common people, including rural residents. Between the BPA, which built the main power grid (and marketed the new energy), and the Rural Electrification Administration co-ops, which extended lines to new customers in the rural stretches of the Northwest, the promise was eventually fulfilled.

ORIGINAL TITLE: "Mile an' a Half from th' End of My Line"

MELODY: "Cumberland Gap"

RECORDINGS: Not recorded for the BPA in any form; recorded commercially for Moe Asch between 1946–47; the same version also appears on the *Columbia River Collection* (Rounder, 1987)

New Found Land

This is one of two songs not included in the recovered BPA manuscripts, which contained only twenty-four of Guthrie's twenty-six Columbia River songs. The two songs—"Grand Coulee Powder Monkey" and "New Found Land"—are speculative, but since the time of Bill Murlin's research, which produced a songbook (*Roll On Columbia: The Columbia River Songs*) and an album (*Columbia River Collection*), the two additional songs have never been refuted. The themes of land reclamation, electrification, and living happily in a land of plenty in "New Found Land" indicate that Guthrie wrote the song as part of the Columbia River song cycle. It was eventually recorded by Moe Asch in New York after Woody's return from his second visit to the Northwest in 1947, and appears on *Ballads from the Dust Bowl* and another release from the 1960s called *Bonneville Dam & Other Columbia River Songs* (Verve Folkways, 1965), further strengthening its case as a Columbia River song. The simplistic tune is based on the "Buffalo Gals" melody.

MELODY: Variant of "Buffalo Gals" and the children's song "This Old Man"

RECORDINGS: Not recorded for the BPA in any form; recorded commercially for Moe Asch in 1947; appeared on *Ballads from the Dust Bowl* (Disc, 1947); the same version also appears on the *Columbia River Collection* (Rounder, 1987)

Out Past the End of the Line

This is another testimonial song of how electricity can benefit the common man and individual farming families. Not to be confused with "End of My Line," "Out Past the End of the Line" uses the melody of "Goin' Down the Road Feeling Bad," a song well associated with Guthrie.

MELODY: "Goin' Down the Road Feeling Bad"

RECORDINGS: Never recorded

Song of the Grand Coulee Dam

This is another discovery from Bill Murlin's research in the 1980s when he solicited information from retired BPA employees regarding Woody Guthrie's employment with the agency. This song, along with "Ramblin' Blues" and "It Takes a Married Man to Sing a Worried Song," was donated by former BPA employee Ralph Bennett who had two other similar "duo-disc" acetate copies that he made from originals of Guthrie BPA recordings during his time at the agency in the late 1940s. All original BPA recordings have been lost. This song hits on familiar themes of a "planned promised land," building dams, hydropower, and the higher purpose of the Columbia River projects.

ALTERNATE TITLE: "Way Up in That Northwest"

MELODY: "On Top of Old Smokey"

RECORDINGS: 1941 BPA acetate copy recovered; available on the *Columbia River Collection* (Rounder, 1988); never recorded commercially

It Takes a Married Man to Sing a Worried Song

This is another song not related to the Columbia River projects but one that Guthrie submitted to the BPA. It's an old song adapted from "Worried Man Blues" lyrically, but uses the melody of "Cannonball Blues." It's quite possibly inspired by Guthrie's crumbling marriage at the time. He and his wife, Mary, separated as soon as the BPA appointment ended, and Woody hitchhiked to New York City while Mary stayed the summer in Portland. They divorced two years later in 1943.

MELODY: "Cannonball Blues"

RECORDINGS: 1941 BPA acetate copy recovered; available on the *Columbia River Collection* (Rounder, 1988)

Eleckatricity and All

One of the more obscure Columbia River songs, about a woman who wants to marry a longshoreman and anticipates the benefits of electricity and all that comes with a modern lifestyle. It doesn't get much rosier than this in terms of "planned promised land" rhetoric and optimistic tone. It's surprising that a demo was not made of this song at the BPA in 1941, as its message seems to hit the mark for what Kahn had in mind for his movie, *The Columbia*.

MELODY: Variant of "I Love Little Willie"

RECORDINGS: Never recorded

Ballad of Jackhammer John

This song is a colorful addition to the great legion of American folk heroes that includes John Henry, Paul Bunyan, and Driller Drake. Guthrie's Jackhammer John is affirmation of the character Woody believed was inherent in working-class people. It's the only Columbia River song that mentions the Tennessee Valley Authority, the forerunner to the Columbia River projects in terms of public works initiated by FDR's New Deal, and is not to be confused with "Jackhammer John" or any "Jackhammer Blues" songs previously mentioned. The melody is from the traditional song "House of the Rising Sun" (as identified by Pete Seeger), but here Guthrie reimagined the actual House of the Rising Sun as a tavern card game in which the legends of labor compete with each other over who's the hardest working. Other characters include the "Prettiest Girl in Red, White, and Blue" who serves as the dealer.

MELODY: "House of the Rising Sun"

RECORDINGS: Never recorded

Talkin' Blues

This is a song about the difficulties of dry farming written prior to Guthrie's Portland experience but was submitted to fulfill his song-a-day requirement.

STYLE: "Talking Blues"

RECORDINGS: Never recorded

Lumber Is King

Guthrie submitted five songs without music. In the mid-1980s, Pete Seeger identified the melodies he suspected Woody to have used or wrote new music to the lyrics. In this case Seeger wrote original music to a twenty-four-verse monumental story of what lumbering and mining might look like one hundred years in the future.

MELODY: Unknown; Pete Seeger wrote original musical notation in the 1980s

RECORDINGS: Never recorded

Portland Town to Klamath Falls

This is the story of a Dust Bowl migrant landing in Oregon. Pete Seeger identified the melody.

MELODY: "Crawdad Song"

RECORDINGS: Never recorded

Grand Coulee Powder Monkey

This is one of two songs not included in the BPA manuscripts. It was published in the 1963 songbook *The Nearly Complete Collection of Woody Guthrie Songs*, and it's considered a Columbia River song because of its title and subject matter. A "powder monkey" used explosives to break rocks at the dam site.

MELODY: "Brown's Ferry Blues"

RECORDINGS: Never recorded

Guys on the Grand Coulee Dam

Guthrie name-drops dam workers, including friends and relatives, in this song about hard work on the dam projects. Pete Seeger identified the melody.

MELODY: "Widdicombe Fair"

RECORDINGS: Never recorded

White Ghost Train

This is a train song with little relation to the Columbia River projects. Pete Seeger identified the tune as "Wabash Cannonball," a favorite melody of Guthrie.

MELODY: "Wabash Cannonball"

RECORDINGS: Never recorded

BLUE LAKE GRAND COULEE OF WASH.

BIBLIOGRAPHY

Bernstein, Irving. "Americans in Depression and War." US Department of Labor. Accessed March 5, 2015. www.dol.gov/dol/aboutdol/history/chapter5.htm.

Bonneville Power Administration press release, October 7, 1987.

Bonneville Power Administration letter requesting paperwork from Guthrie, Woody Guthrie Archives, May 1, 1941.

Buehler, Elmer, interviewed by Greg Vandy.

Buehler, Elmer, interviewed by Michael Madjic.

Buehler, Elmer. Written recollections, BPA Library.

Burke, Libby, e-mail message to Greg Vandy.

Caravan. August–September 1958.

"Columbia Basin Project." US Department of the Interior, Bureau of Land Reclamation. 2012. http://www.usbr.gov/projects/Project.jsp?proj_Name=Columbia%20Basin%20Project.

Cray, Ed. "The Performer and the Promoter" in *The Life, Music and Thought of Woody Guthrie*, ed. John S. Partington. Burlington, VT: Ashgate Pub Co., 2011.

Cray, Ed. *Ramblin' Man: The Life and Times of Woody Guthrie*. New York: W. W. Norton, 2004.

Duncan, David James. *My Story as Told by Water*. San Francisco: Sierra Club Books, 2001.

Egan, Timothy. "Portland Journal: For $266, Verse Low and Lofty By Guthrie." *New York Times*, August 4, 1991. Accessed March 23, 2015.

"Electricity in the Limelight: The Federal Theatre Project Takes on the Power Industry." New Deal Network. Accessed March 4, 2015. http://newdeal.feri.org/power/essay01.htm.

Emmons, Della Florence Gould. *Northwest History in Action*. Minneapolis, MN: T. S. Denison, 1960.

Flanagan, Hallie. *Arena: The Story of the Federal Theatre*. New York: Limelight Editions, 1985.

Grand Coulee Dam. Directed by Stephen Ives. PBS Distribution, 2012. Film.

Guthrie, Arlo. Facebook post, March 18, 2015. https://www.facebook.com/arloguthrie/posts/10155379478995195?fref=nf&pnref=story.

Guthrie, Woody and Alan Lomax. *Woody Guthrie: American Radical Patriot*. Rounder, 2013.

Guthrie, Woody. Letter to Alan Lomax. Woody Guthrie Archives, February 21, 1941.

Guthrie, Woody. Letter to Alan Lomax. Woody Guthrie Archives, undated.

Guthrie, Woody. Letter to Elizabeth and Harold Ambellan. Woody Guthrie Archives, June 10, 1941.

Guthrie, Woody. Letter to Michael Loring. Woody Guthrie Archives, July 9, 1948.

Guthrie, Woody. Letter to Mill Lampell. Woody Guthrie Archives, April 9, 1941.

Guthrie, Woody. Letter to Mill Lampell. Woody Guthrie Archives, September 9, 1941.

Guthrie, Woody. Letter to Moe Asch. Woody Guthrie Archives, April 22, 1947.

Guthrie, Woody. Letter to the Almanac Singers. Woody Guthrie Archives, July 8, 1941.

Guthrie, Woody. *Roll On Columbia: The Columbia River Songs*. Portland, OR: BPA, 1988.

Guthrie, Woody. *The Nearly Complete Collection of Woody Guthrie Folk Songs*. Ludlow Music, 1963.

Harden, Blaine. *A River Lost*. New York: W. W. Norton, 1996.

Harvey, Todd, interviewed by Greg Vandy and Daniel Person, February 25, 2015.

Herman, Arthur. *Freedom's Forge: How American Business Produced Victory in World War II*. New York: Random House, 2012.

International Union of Mine, Mill and Smelter Workers. *Official Proceedings of the 50th Convention of the International Union of Mine, Mill and Smelter Workers*. Ithaca, NY: Cornell University, 1955.

Kahn, Stephen, interviewed by Michael Madjic.

The Columbia: America's Greatest Power Stream. Directed by Stephen Kahn. BPA Motion Picture Information, 1949. Film.

Kazin, Michael. *American Dreamers*. New York: Vintage, 2011.

Klein, Joe. *Woody Guthrie: A Life*. Crystal Lake, IL: Delta, 1980.

Lomax, Alan, interviewed by Richard A. Reuss. Richard Reuss Collection, Indiana University Archives, August 29, 1966.

Lowitt, Richard. *The New Deal and the West*. Norman, OK: University of Oklahoma Press, 1984.

Macnab, Gordon. "Folk Craze Revives Columbia Dam Songs." *Associated Press*, October 17, 1963.

McGregor, Michael. "The Vanport Flood & Racial Change in Portland." Oregon History Project. 2003. www.ohs.org/education/oregonhistory/learning_center/dspresource.cfm?resource_ID=000B-C26B-EE5A-1E47-AE5A80B05272FE9F. Accessed March 15, 2015.

Murlin, Bill, interviewed by Greg Vandy and Daniel Person, April 21, 2014; May 5, 2014; March 16–17, 2015; and March 25, 2015.

Murlin, Bill. *Roll On Columbia: The Columbia River Songs*. Portland, OR: Bonnevile Power Administration, 1987.

Murlin, Bill. Letter to Merle Meacham. September 1, 1983.

Nate, Richard. "'Pastures of Plenty': Woody Guthrie and the New Deal" in *The Life, Music and Thought of Woody Guthrie*, ed. John S. Partington. Burlington, VT: Ashgate Pub Co., 2011.

Neuberger, Richard L. *Our Promised Land*. New York: Macmillan, 1938.

Norwood, Gus. *Columbia River Power for the People*. Portland, OR: Bonneville Power Administration, 1981.

Person, Daniel. "Forgotten Sacrifices: Grand Coulee Memorial Found in Colville." *Spokesman-Review*, May 24, 2014.

Pitzer, Paul C. *Grand Coulee: Harnessing a Dream*. Pullman, WA: Washington State University Press, 1994.

Pitzer, Paul, interviewed by Greg Vandy and Daniel Person, March 17, 2015.

Place, Jeffrey. *Woody at 100: The Woody Guthrie Centennial Collection*. Washington, DC: Smithsonian Folkways Recordings, 2012.

Platt, Susan Noyes. *Art & Politics in the 1930s*. New York: Midmarch Arts Press, 1999.

"Power from the Columbia River." BPA poster, circa 1942.

"Power Trust Takes Beating in W.P.A. Play," *Seattle Daily Times*, July 8, 1937.

Quart, Leonard. "Frank Capra and the Popular Front" in *American Media and Mass Culture*, ed. Donald Lazere. Oakland, CA: University of California Press, 1987.

Reuss, Richard A., and Joanne C. Reuss. *American Folk Music and Left-Wing Politics: 1927–1957*. Lanham, MD: Scarecrow Press, 2000.

Reuss, Richard. Letter to Bill Murlin. Indiana University Archives, May 22, 1981.

Ritchie, Fiona, and Doug Orr. *Wayfaring Strangers: The Musical Journey from Scotland and Ulster to Appalachia*. Chapel Hill, NC: University of North Carolina Press, 2014.

Roll On Columbia: Woody Guthrie and the Bonneville Power Administration. Directed by Michael Madjic. University of Oregon, 2000. Film.

Roll On, Columbia: Woody Guthrie and the Columbia River Songs. Directed by Michael O'Rourke. Oregon Public Broadcasting, 2009. Film.

Roosevelt, Franklin D. "Address at Bonneville Dam." New Deal Network, September 28, 1937. http://newdeal.feri.org/speeches/1937c.htm.

Roosevelt, Franklin D. "Inaugural Gubernatorial Address." New Deal Network, January 1, 1929. www.fdrlibrary.marist.edu/education/resources/pdfs/fdrstandard1.pdf. Accessed February 29, 2015.

Roosevelt, Franklin D. "Portland Speech: Public Utilities Hydro-Electric Power. New Deal Network, September 21, 1932. http://newdeal.feri.org/speeches/1932a.htm. Accessed February 29, 2015.

Roosevelt, Franklin D. "The Forgotten Man." New Deal Network, April 7, 1932. http://newdeal.feri.org/speeches/1932c.htm. Accessed March 5, 2015.

Ross, J. D. "The Federal Power Plants and Public Power." *Public Utilities Fortnightly*, June 9, 1938.

Santelli, Robert and Emily Davidson. *Hard Travelin': The Life and Legacy of Woody Guthrie*. Middletown, CT: Wesleyan University Press, 1999.

Seeger, Pete, interviewed by Michael Madjic.

Tate, Cassandra. "Native Americans Begin 'Ceremony of Tears' for Kettle Falls on June 14, 1940." HistoryLink.org, 2005. www.historylink.org/index.cfm?DisplayPage=output.cfm&file_id=7276. Accessed March 16, 2015.

The Bonneville Project Personnel Action. Portland, OR: Bonneville Power Administration, April, 23 1941.

The Dust Bowl. Directed by Ken Burns. PBS Distribution, 2012. Film.

"The Photography Project." *Celebrating New Deal Arts & Culture*. University of Indiana, 2009. http://www.indiana.edu/~libsalc/newdeal/photo.html.

The Plow That Broke the Plains. Directed by Pare Lorentz. US Resettlement Administration, 1936. Film.

The Richmond Organization, e-mail message to Greg Vandy, first recordings of "Roll On, Columbia."

The River. Directed by Pare Lorentz. Farm Security Administration, 1938. Film.

The Weavers Reunion at Carnegie Hall: 1963. Recorded May 2–3, 1963.

Tollefson, Gene. "Background on Historic Motion Pictures." Internal memo to Administrator Sterling Munro. Portland, OR: Bonneville Power Administration, 1980.

Tollefson, Gene. *BPA and the Struggle for Power at Cost.* Portland, OR: Bonneville Power Administration, 1987.

"US Energy Information Administration." EIA. www.eia.gov/electricity/monthly/epm_table_grapher.cfm?t=epmt_5_06_a.

Wallace, Henry. "The Singing People." *The New Republic*, June 28, 1948.

White, Richard. *The Organic Machine: The Remaking of the Columbia.* New York: Hill and Wang, 1996.

The Upper Grand Coulee near Coulee Dam (Central Washington)

© 1947
WESTERN
SOUVENIRS
543

PHOTO CREDITS

Page 46: Original typed lyric, "Jackhammer John" by Woody Guthrie ©
Woody Guthrie Publications, Inc. Courtesy of the Ralph Rinzler Folklife
Archives and Collections, Smithsonian Institution

Page 51: Alan Lomax Collection, courtesy of the Prints and Photographs
Division, Library of Congress

Page 52: Courtesy of the Geer family

Page 59: Courtesy of Woody Guthrie Publications, Inc.

Page 62: Original typed lyric, "Pastures of Plenty" by Woody Guthrie ©
Woody Guthrie Publications, Inc. Courtesy of the Ralph Rinzler Folklife
Archives and Collections, Smithsonian Institution

Page 66: Poster by Vera Bock, courtesy of the Library of Congress

Page 68: Library of Congress

Page 81: Map by the Lindgren Brothers, courtesy of the Library
of Congress

Page 82: Bureau Of Land Reclamation, courtesy of Grant County
Historical Museum

Page 90: Original lyric, "Washington Talking Blues" by Woody Guthrie ©
Woody Guthrie Publications, Inc. Courtesy of the Ralph Rinzler Folklife
Archives and Collections, Smithsonian Institution

Page 102: Postcard by Wesley Andrews Co, Portland, Oregon

Page 105: Photograph by Arthur Rothstein, courtesy of the Library
of Congress

Page 114: Original typed lyric, "Roll Columbia" by Woody Guthrie ©
Woody Guthrie Publications, Inc. Courtesy of the Ralph Rinzler Folklife
Archives and Collections, Smithsonian Institution

Photo Credits

INDEX

Note: Photographs are indicated by *italics*.

A

albums, 59, *59*, 124, *124*, 139, 140–141, *142*, 143
Army Corps of Engineers, 78
Asch, Moe, 54, 122–124, *122*, 141

B

Back Where I Come From, *9*, 59, 61
"Ballad of Jackhammer John," 142, 169
Ballads from the Dust Bowl, 124, *124*, 141
Banks, Frank A., *36*
Bennett, Ralph, 122, 138–139, 153
"Biggest Thing That Man Has Ever Done," *xvi*, 107–108, 115, 119, 121, 139, 160
Bonneville Dam, 2–3, 39–40, *40*, 84–85, 87, 108
Bonneville Power Administration, *92*
  anti-public-power backlash, 143–144, 153
  creation of, 2–3, 40–41, 85
  hiring of Guthrie, 10, *11*, 12–13, 91–113
  promotion of public power, 3–5, *3*, *38*, 41–45, 85–87, *86*, *88*
  war effort, 2, 87, *88*, 117
  See also Columbia River songs; Kahn, Stephen
Bound for Glory (Guthrie), 7, *17*
Buehler, Elmer, xii, 101–106, *101*, 108–109, 143–144
Burke, J. Frank, 25, 27–28, 29, 31

C

Cahill, Holger, 65, 67, 70
Celilo Falls, 109, *109*
Clapp, Billy, 77
Cold War, 60, 144, 153
Columbia: America's Greatest Power Stream, The, 15, 93, 115, 117–121, *120*, 135, 139, 143–145
Columbia River Collection, The, 139, 140–141, *142*, 143
Columbia River songs, ix, xi–xiv, 147–148, 153
  on *The Columbia* soundtrack, 119, 121, 139
  discography, 159–171
  Guthrie's writing of, 99–113
  popularization of, 121–129
  recordings of, 111, 115, 117, 122, 124, 129, 138–145
  research on, by Murlin, xi–xii, 134–145

"Columbia Talkin' Blues," 108, 111, 124, 134, 139, *146*, 164
"Columbia Waters," 139, 165
Communist Party, 29–30, 68–70, 153
copyrights, 140
Corn Cob Trio, 24
Crissman, Maxine "Lefty Lou," *12*, 26, *26*

D

Dalles Dam, The, 109, *109*
"Do Re Mi," 27
Dunn, Donald, 149–150
Dust Bowl, 21–24
  See also migrant farmers
Dust Bowl Ballads, 59, *59*
Dylan, Bob, 133

E

"Eleckatricity and All," 108, *158*, 169
electricity. *See* hydroelectricity
Elliott, Ramblin' Jack, 133, 134, *137*
"End of My Line," 108, 124, 166

F

farmers, migrant. *See*
  migrant farmers
Farm-in-a-Day demonstration
  project, 149 150
Farm Security Administration
  (FSA), 28–29, *29*, 53, 64, 67
Federal Art Project, 65, *66*, 67
Federal One (Federal Project No. 1), 65, 70
Federal Theatre Project, 70–73, *71*
folk art, 4–5, 63–73
folk music, 50–55, 131

Forrest Theatre concert, 47–56, *48*

G

Geer, Will, 29, 31, *52*, 53
"God Bless America," 52–53
"Good Morning, Mr. Captain." *See*
  "Columbia Waters"
Grand Coulee Dam, *116*, 124, 151
  construction of, *36*, 39–40, 79–84, 87, *107*, 121
  Guthrie's support for, 74, 76, 89, 106–108
  See also Bonneville Power
    Administration; hydroelectricity;
    irrigation project
"Grand Coulee Dam" (song), *32*, 121, 133, 139, 161
"Grand Coulee Powder Monkey," 141–142, 171
Grange, the, 37, 39, 104
Grapes of Wrath, The (Steinbeck), 4–5, *4*, 7, 28, 47, 58, 95
Great Depression, 2, 63, 64
Guthrie, Charley (father), 16, 18–19, 20, 21
Guthrie, Clara (sister), 20, 21
Guthrie, Jack (cousin), 25–26
Guthrie, Mary (wife), 6, *11*, *12*, 16, 24, 25, 60–61, 99–100, 112 113
Guthrie, Nora (mother), 16, 19, 20
Guthrie, Woody, 15–16
  birth and early life in Okemah,
    Oklahoma, 16–21, *17*
  in Columbia, California, 12–13
  in Dust Bowl, 21–24
  hired for BPA film project, 10, *11*, 12–13, 91–113

illness and death, 131, 133

leftist politics, 26–31, 52–53, 60, 153

legend, growth of, 133–134

in Los Angeles, 5–7, 10–12, 25–31

in New York City, 7–8, *9*, 47–61, 115, 117

in Pampas, Texas, 21, 23–25, *23*

radio programs, 7–8, *9*, 25–28, *26*, 31, 57, 58, 59–61, 121–122

support for Columbia River projects, 28–29, 74, 76, 89, 106–108

World War II, 31, 107–108, 117

See also Columbia River songs; migrant farmers

"Guys on the Grand Coulee Dam," 107, 142, 171

H

Hanford Site, 151

"Hard Travelin'," *14*, 111, 121, 124, 100

Here Comes Woody and Lefty Lou, 26, *26*

Houston, Cisco, 177

Hydro, 42, *43*, 102, 119, 144

hydroelectricity, 2–5, 33–45, 84–89, 107–108, 117, 151

"hysterical maps," 81, *81*

I

irrigation project, 73–80, 83–84, 105–106, 121, 148–151, *149*, *150*, *152*

"It Takes a Married Man to Sing a Worried Song," 111, 139, 168

J

"Jackhammer Blues," *46*, 111, 139, 161

K

Kahn, Stephen, 3–5, 41–42, *42*, 44–45, 93–95, 98, 100, 102, 110, 111, 115, 117–121, 144, 153

KFVD radio station, 7, 25–28, *26*, 29, 57

L

"Liberty ships," 1–2, *2*, 117

Light, 28

Lomax, Alan, 5, *6*, 7, 53–59, *53*, 61, 93, 143, 153

Lomax, John A., *51*, 54–55

Lorentz, Pare, 44

Loring, Michael, 124–125, *126*, 127, *128*, 153

Lost Lake, *102*, 103

"Lumber Is King," 142, 170

M

Macnab, Gordon, 138–139

Meacham, Merle, 138–139

migrant farmers, 27–30, *28*, *29*, *30*, 105–106, 121, 148

Model Tobacco Company, 7–8, 60–61

Murlin, Bill, xi–xii, 134–145, *137*

N

Native Americans, 73–74, 89, 101, 108–110, *109*, 151–152
New Deal, 4, 28–29, *29*, 37, 39–40, 44, 64–67, 70–73, 79, 83–85, 87
"New Found Land," 124, 141–142, 167

O

"Oklahoma Hills," 26
"Oregon Trail," 124, *130*, 164
"Out Past the End of the Line," 167

P

"Pastures of Plenty," *62*, 95, 106, 115, 119, 121, 124, 133, 139, 140–141, 162
patriotism, xiv, 68, 98, 107–108
Pipe Smoking Time, 7–8, 61
"planned promised land," 79, 83–84
Pledge of Allegiance, 30, *31*
politics, 26–31, 52–53, 60, 153
Popular Front, 68–70
Portland, Oregon, 1–2, *2*, 99–100, 112
"Portland Town." *See* "Ramblin' Blues"
"Portland Town to Klamath Falls," 142, 170
Power, *35*, 70–73, *71*
"Pretty Boy Floyd," 55–56
Prohibition, 21
public power. *See* hydroelectricity
public utility districts (PUDs), 39, 41, 42, 44, 85, 151

R

radio programs, 7–8, *9*, 25–28, *26*, 29, 31, 57, 58, 59–61, 121–122
"Ramblin' Blues," 139, 165
"Ramblin' Round," 124, 166
Raver, Paul, 94
recordings, 57–59, 61, 111, 115, 117, 122, 129, 138–145
See also albums
religion, 30–31
Reuss, Richard, 135–136, 137
Robbin, Ed, 29
Rogers, Will, 54
"Roll, Columbia, Roll," 108, *114*, 115, 119, 129, 139, 163
"Roll On, Columbia," *x*, xii, 100–101, 108, 121, 124–129, *126*, 136, 138, 139, 159
Roll On, Columbia: The Columbia River Songs, 141–143, *141*
Roosevelt, Franklin D., 2–3, 33–37, *36*, 39–40, 64–65, 78, 83–85
Ross, J. D., 37, 40–41, *41*, 85, 94, 117

S

salmon, 73–74, 89, 109–110, *109*, 152
"scatteration technique," 110, 122
Seeger, Charles, 53, 54
Seeger, Pete, 53, 54, 115, 124–125, *126*, 141, 142, 153
Socialist Party, 18
"So Long, It's Been Good to Know Yuh," 7, 24
songbooks, 124–125, *126*, 141–143, *141*
"Song of the Grand Coulee Dam," 139, 168

Spokane, Washington, 122, *123*
Steinbeck, John, 4–5, 7, 28, 47, 58
Sullivan's Gulch, 2, 41

T

"Talkin' Blues," 170
  See also "Columbia Talkin' Blues"
Tennessee Valley Authority, 40, 44,
  70 73, *71*
"This Land is Your Land," 5, 53,
  102–103
"Tom Joad," 7, 58, 95

V

Vanport Flood, 118–119, *110*
Von Fritsch, Gunther, 10, *11*, 42, 45,
  93, 117

W

Wallace, Henry, 125, 127
Washington State Grange, 39, 79
"Washington Talkin' Blues," *90*,
  105–106, 139, 163
"Way Up in that Northwest." *See*
  "Song of the Grand Coulee Dam"
"White Ghost Train," 142, 171
Woods, Rufus, 77–79
"Woody Sez" column, 29–30, *31*
Works Progress Administration
  (WPA), *35*, 65–67, *66*, 70–73, *71*
World War I, 19
World War II, 1–2, *2*, 31, 87, *88*,
  107–108, 117–118, 148

GRAND COULEE DAM   LENGTH AT TOP - 4,300 ft   POWER PLANT 2,700,000 H.P.
              HEIGHT - 550 ft   CREATES LAKE 151 MILES LONG
              WIDTH AT BASE - 500 ft   WATERFALL TWICE THE HEIGHT OF NIAGARA

ABOUT THE AUTHORS

GREG VANDY lives in Seattle, Washington, with his wife and two dogs, Jackson and Katie Mae. He's been the host of *The Roadhouse* on KEXP-FM Seattle since 2000, and is a lifelong supporter of non-commercial community radio. In addition to being a DJ and a content consultant for various media and music festivals, he publishes *American Standard Time*, a blog devoted to American music and vintage lifestyles. This is his first book.

Ccco Foto

DANIEL PERSON was born and raised in Helena, Montana, just over the Continental Divide from the Columbia River watershed. His work has appeared in *High Country News*, *Cowboys & Indians*, *Seattle Weekly*, *Montana Quarterly*, and *Outside Online*. Today he is the news editor of *Seattle Weekly*. He lives in Tacoma, another public power community.

Jose Trujillo

Take it easy
But take it.
Woody Guthrie

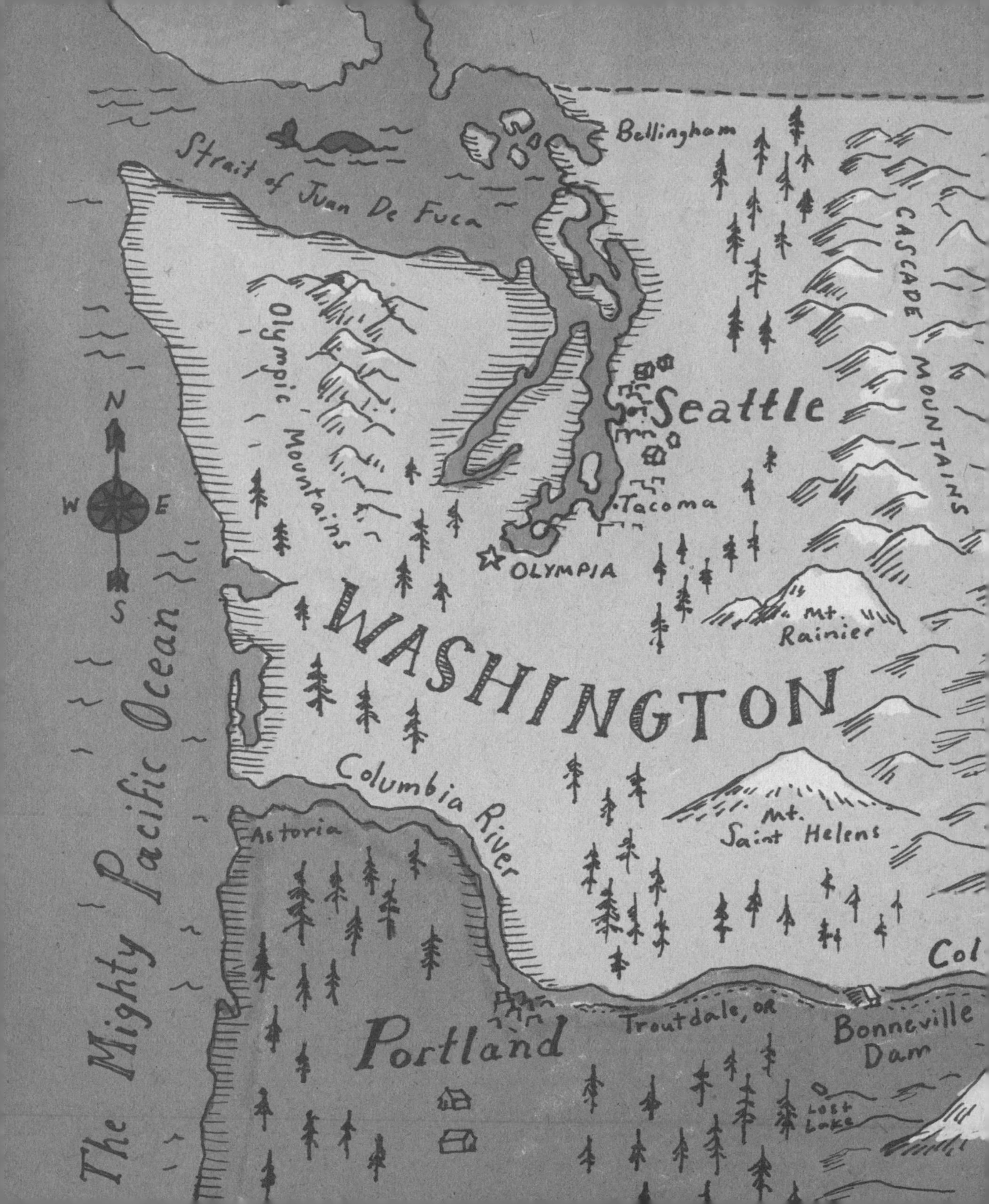
Strait of Juan De Fuca
Bellingham
Olympic Mountains
Seattle
CASCADE MOUNTAINS
N
W
E
S
Tacoma
OLYMPIA
The Mighty Pacific Ocean
WASHINGTON
Mt. Rainier
Columbia River
Astoria
Mt. Saint Helens
Col
Troutdale, OR
Bonneville Dam
Portland
Lost Lake